Starting an English Literature Degree

The **English Subject Centre** serves and supports learning and teaching in English Literature, English Language and Creative Writing across UK higher education. It provides events, publications, resources and a website www.english.heacademy.ac.uk for lecturers and also two web resources for students: Why Study English? www.whystudyenglish.ac.uk and After English – thinking about your future as an English graduate www.english.heacademy.ac.uk/afterenglish/

Starting an English Literature Degree

ANDREW GREEN

palgrave
macmillan

First published 2009 by
PALGRAVE MACMILLAN

Palgrave Macmillan in the UK is an imprint of Macmillan Publishers Limited, registered in England, company number 785998, of Houndmills, Basingstoke, Hampshire RG21 6XS.

Palgrave Macmillan in the US is a division of St Martin's Press LLC, 175 Fifth Avenue, New York, NY 10010.

Palgrave Macmillan is the global academic imprint of the above companies and has companies and representatives throughout the world.

Palgrave® and Macmillan® are registered trademarks in the United States, the United Kingdom, Europe and other countries.

ISBN: 978-0-230-21183-4 paperback

This book is printed on paper suitable for recycling and made from fully managed and sustained forest sources. Logging, pulping and manufacturing processes are expected to conform to the environmental regulations of the country of origin.

A catalogue record for this book is available from the British Library.

A catalog record for this book is available from the Library of Congress.

10 9 8 7 6 5 4 3 2 1
18 17 16 15 14 13 12 11 10 09

Printed and bound in Great Britain by
CPI Antony Rowe, Chippenham and Eastbourne

Nathaniel and Oliver, this one is for you. Who knows, maybe one day you'll need it.

Contents

List of Figures

Foreword

The experience of studying English Literature at university is not the same as the experience of studying the subject at school. The purpose of this book is to introduce you to what the study of English Literature at university is about and to help you build useful bridges between what you did at A level and what you will need to do if you are to succeed in your studies at university. It is divided into two sections: the first, a brief overview of how you can use your study of English Literature at A level to prepare yourself for the demands of university study; the second, an in-depth exploration of the demands of university study in English Literature and how you can most effectively manage this.

Acknowledgements

Many people's help has been willingly given and gratefully received in the writing of this book. I would like to acknowledge all of them with thanks. The following in particular deserve mention:

The English and Media Centre (www.englishmedia.co.uk) for permission to use in Chapters 1, 6 and 7 materials originally published by the author in e-magazine: 'Going to study English Lit?', first published in e-magazine 15, 2002, 'Theoretically speaking', first published in e-magazine 41, 2008 and 'Philip Larkin, Jazz and *The Whitsun Weddings*', first published in e-magazine December 2004.

Philip Allan Updates for permission to use materials originally published by the author in *Gothic: Frankenstein and Wuthering Heights, Songs of Innocence and of Experience, Frankenstein, The Whitsun Weddings* and *High Windows*.

Dr Ewan Fernie, Professor Adam Roberts, Professor Robert Eaglestone, and Dr William Leahy, who generously gave of their time.

Professor Ben Knights and Jane Gawthrope of the English Subject Centre at whose suggestion the commission for this book came about.

Professor Tim Middleton of the Joseph Conrad Society for permission to use materials published on the Joseph Conrad Society website.

Nikki, who has supported me in ways too many to mention.

1 Initial bearings

By the end of this chapter you will have considered:

- what to think about when selecting a university;
- your experience of English Literature at A level, IB or Access;
- the subject knowledge you have gained to date;
- what abilities are necessary to succeed at university;
- the nature of study at university;
- relations with academic staff;
- working at university.

INTRODUCTION

The fact that you are reading this book probably means one of two things. Either you are a student who has recently begun studying English Literature at university or you are a student thinking about doing so. In either case you are to be congratulated. Welcome to the exciting world of English Literature. There is no other subject that offers its students such a world of possibilities. Up until now you will have studied a handful of literary texts: a few for your GCSEs and slightly more for A Level, International Baccalaureate (IB) or an Access course. The fun really starts at university, though. So far your study of English Literature has been one part of academic studies, combined with courses in History, Music, Modern Foreign Languages, Geography or Religious Studies, perhaps. Maybe some of you will even have studied one or two of the sciences or Mathematics. English Literature has been only a part of your academic focus. From the point you enter university, however, it will form the major focus of your work.

And what a great thing it is to focus on. To spend three years (and possibly more) of your life studying a selection of the greatest works of literature ever produced is both an honour and a pleasure. It is now many years since I began my own English Literature degree, but I can still remember the excitement of following the course. The pleasures and memories of it have lasted with me throughout my life. It had its difficult moments for certain, and there were times when it was very hard work. Many hours of midnight oil (and early morning oil) were burnt in order to meet essay deadlines and to ensure that reading was completed in time for lectures and seminars, but every minute and hour was worth it.

Of course, this book cannot cover every eventuality, but a good place to start is by thinking about what factors you should consider when you are selecting where you will study.

SELECTING A UNIVERSITY

There are several important issues to consider here:

- course content;
- staff expertise;
- course delivery;
- location.

Course content. Every university course in English Literature is different, as it should be. Courses are not dictated as they were at school or college, by a National Curriculum or by exam syllabuses. University departments are much freer to devise their own courses than are schools and FE colleges. University English Literature courses will reflect a range of different influences, including the academic expertise of the teaching staff. You will almost certainly be able to study Shakespeare and the other major figures from the literary canon – Dickens, Austen, Chaucer, Conrad and so on. You will also have the opportunity to study a much wider range of literature, however. Maybe literatures in translation, Old English and Norse literature, specialist author papers, literary theory or genre papers (e.g. Gothic fiction or science fiction). You may

2

also have the chance to take modules looking at film adaptations of literature, performance, English Language or creative writing. The vast range of possibilities on offer means it is very important to look closely at what particular universities offer. It is important that you choose an institution on the basis of its course rather than exclusively on its name. An institution may be very prestigious, but if it does not offer courses that you find stimulating, your three years as an undergraduate will not be fulfilling.

Staff expertise. It may be that you already have a clear picture of what you wish to study. You may, for example, have a burning desire to study the works of Salman Rushdie, Restoration theatre, literature and religion, or a particular literary genre. If this is the case, it would be well worth your while to look into the research interests and reputations of the academic staff in the departments you are thinking of applying to. Most departmental websites will have staff biographies, including research interests, lists of publications, conference addresses and so on. This will give you some insight into where you will gain the most innovative and authoritative teaching in the areas of your own personal interest. If you are trying to map out an academic pathway for your career – thinking of going on to Masters and even PhD level – this kind of strategic thinking can be very important.

Course delivery. It is not only courses that vary from one place to another. Teaching arrangements, the number of taught hours per week, numbers of assignments, means and variety of assessment type, possibility of undertaking work placement, use of virtual learning environments, the range and type of reading required may all vary from institution to institution. Again it is important to look carefully at these details before you apply for university. You need to think carefully about whether the practical arrangements for the delivery of particular courses you are applying for actually suit what you want and need.

Location. It is not only in the property market that location matters. The choice of university you make is not solely academic. Your choice of university is also a choice of where you will be living. The quality of the course may well be of great significance, but so too is your happiness with where you live. You should think carefully about the following questions. Is it a campus university? Is it urban? Is it rural? What is the transport like? How near to home is it? Do you want to live that near to (or far from) home? Is accommodation available in halls of residence? If so, for how many years? What other accommodation is available for students? What is the local area like? What leisure and social facilities are there? Is catering good? These questions may seem obvious, but they are also very important. Especially in the rush of clearing, or in the excitement at being offered a place, it is all too easy to overlook practicalities like this and to end up unhappy.

English Literature degrees and the universities that offer them vary widely. That said, however, it is possible to draw some useful generalisations about what the study of English Literature at university entails, and I trust that this book manages to capture the spirit of English Literature at university. It aims to introduce you to how the subject you are going to study (or thinking of studying) is related to, but also different from English Literature at A Level, IB or Access levels. If you are to make an effective transition from your A level, IB or Access course to university, it is important that you understand how the subject and its emphases change between school and university.

This opening chapter, therefore, will introduce you to a set of practical issues about how universities work and what English Literature at university comprises. Throughout the book you will find lots of practical examples and activities to help you understand how you can work most effectively during your degree and to get you thinking about how your studies so far have (and how they have not) prepared you for what you will face.

YOUR EXPERIENCE SO FAR

It is important before you begin your English Literature degree to think where you are in your understanding of what English Literature is and what you want to gain from studying the subject at university. Your experiences of studying English Literature at GCSE and then at A level, IB or Access level will all have made a significant impact on your views about what the subject of English

Literature is and what the study of it entails. Your studies so far will have instilled in you a set of assumptions and values that you may have to challenge when it comes to studying English Literature for your degree. It is important, therefore, to ask some detailed questions of yourself and your assumptions about what English Literature entails. Think about your most recent experience of studying English Literature, and also what you imagine study at university to be like.

ACTIVITY I

Your experiences so far

Take some space and time to reflect on the questions below. This will be a useful preparation for you as you begin reading this book, and also as you start your English Literature degree. Being able and prepared to challenge your own presuppositions is one of the hallmarks of an effective student, and so it is important to spend time defining what you think English Literature as a subject is, and what your presuppositions about it are.

(1) Jot down some thoughts about your own experiences of English Literature at school. What was it like? Exciting? Challenging? Incomprehensible? Wide and varied? Narrow in range?
(2) How did your teachers make you feel about English Literature? That it was an adventure? That it was approachable? That it was distant? That you were free to 'play' with it? That it was to be revered? That it was about broadening your mind? That it was about passing an exam?
(3) How did your teachers set about teaching you English Literature? Try to remember a range of the pedagogic approaches they adopted.
(4) How do you think the teaching you receive at university will differ from the ways in which you were taught at school?
(5) If you had to sum up what English Literature was 'about' before university, how would you do so?
(6) What do you think English literature is 'about' at university?
(7) What are you hoping to achieve through your study of English Literature at university?

➢

(8) What do you think are the characteristics most important to achieving success in the study of English Literature at university?

(9) Did you study any English Language at A level, either as a separate subject or as part of an English Language and Literature A level? How do you understand the interaction of language and literature in the study of English?

This is the starting point. The answers to these questions will provide you with some key insights into what you are actually expecting of your English Literature degree. How these views and expectations then relate to your study of English Literature at degree level is another matter, and you may well have to change radically some of the assumptions you have brought with you from your previous studies. A clear understanding of these assumptions is very important, as it is difficult to challenge and overcome assumptions you do not even know you hold. Your experience of English Literature so far is the key means you will use to 'read' and come to terms with the new experiences you will gain at university. Your understanding of your new environment will be all the more clear if you know exactly where you are coming from.

AUDITING YOUR KNOWLEDGE

Another useful thing for you to do as you start your degree is to audit your knowledge of literature so far. This will help you to build up a picture of where you stand in terms of your literary knowledge. Below is an activity which will help you to structure your audit of subject knowledge. Be as comprehensive as you can, as it is important that you develop at this stage the fullest picture you can of your subject knowledge and its range. Whenever you come to a new text you 'read' it against the background of all your previous reading. It is therefore important for you to know where your greatest body of knowledge lies and where you need to be doing some preparatory work to catch up and to prepare the ground for new reading and study.

ACTIVITY 2

Auditing your subject knowledge

(1) List of major authors published before 1914

The following list is drawn form the National Curriculum, and therefore represents a set of authors you are likely to have studied.

Major poets pre-1914
Arnold, E. B. Browning, Blake, Emily Bronte, R. Browning, Burns, Byron, Chaucer, Clare, Coleridge, Donne, Dryden, Gray, Herbert, Herrick, Hopkins, Keats, Marvell, Milton, Pope, Rossetti, Shakespeare (sonnets), P. B. Shelley, Spenser, Tennyson, Vaughan, Wordsworth, Wyatt.

Examples of major playwrights
Congreve, Goldsmith, Marlowe, O'Casey, Pinter, Priestley, Shaffer, Shaw, Sheridan, Wilde.

Major fiction writers published before 1914
Austen, Charlotte Bronte, Bunyan, Collins, Conrad, Defoe, Dickens, Conan Doyle, G. Eliot, Fielding, Gaskell, Hardy, James, Mary Shelley, Stevenson, Swift, Trollope, Wells.

- Identify as fully as possible your familiarity with the works of these authors. Do not worry if you have not read much (or anything) by all of them. The purpose of this is to identify constructive areas for development.
- Are there other pre-1914 authors you are familiar with as well as those listed here? Who are they?

(2) Examples of major authors after 1914

Examples of major poets after 1914
Auden, Clarke, Douglas, T. S. Eliot, Fanthorpe, Hardy, Heaney, Hughes, Jennings, Larkin, Owen, Plath, Smith, E. Thomas, R. S. Thomas, Yeats.

Examples of fiction by major writers after 1914
Forster, Golding, Greene, Huxley, Joyce, Lawrence, Mansfield, Orwell, Spark, Trevor, Waugh.

➤

7

- Again, identify as fully as possible your familiarity with these authors.
- In addition, add the names of any others you are familiar with.

(3) *Contemporary authors and authors from other cultures*

- Which contemporary authors and authors from other cultures are you familiar with? This may include literature in translation.

(4) *Literary theory and literary criticism*

- Which literary theorists and critics are you familiar with?

The lists of authors and their works that you have drawn up are the ruler against which you will measure your English Literature course at university. They capture your experience to date of the subject you have opted to read and will be one of the most important means by which you access the texts, authors and issues you now go on to study. You should now use this audit as the basis for developing your subject knowledge.

On the basis of your responses, draw up a target reading list so that you can think about developing a wider range of knowledge you can draw on in your studies.

RANGE OF COVERAGE

English degrees cover a very wide range of content and vary considerably from one institution to another. For this reason, it is very important to check out the details of the courses you are applying for, looking at their compulsory and optional components to make sure that you like their range and content. It is impossible to make generalisations about a 'typical' course. However, modules tend to fall within the following broad categories:

- *author-based courses*, which focus on the works of a single author or a small group of authors (e.g. Shakespeare, Dickens, James, or Coleridge and Wordsworth) – such modules tend, with the exception of Shakespeare, to be optional modules in the second and the third years;

- *period-based courses*, which provide broad coverage of a literary period (e.g. Romantic Literature, Victorian Literature, Modernism);
- *genre-based courses*, which provide the opportunity for detailed study of a particular genre (e.g. Modern Drama, The Gothic Novel, Lyric Poetry);
- *Creative Writing*;
- *English Language* (e.g. Linguistics, Language Acquisition);
- *related subject areas* (e.g. Film Studies, Performance, American Studies);
- *other modules* related to your study of English (e.g. Literary Theory, Academic Practice) are often part of early degree-level study, and sometimes option modules can be drawn from a wider pool of subject areas (e.g. Modern Foreign Languages, other Humanities and Performing Arts subjects).

Undertaking the audit in Activity 2 will help you to think about what your studies to date have prepared you to do and will also focus your mind on what other experiences of English you wish to gain through your study at university. This will be helpful in your selection of course when you are applying and will also help you in your selection of options.

ENGLISH LANGUAGE

You may well have the opportunity, if you wish, to include some study of English Language within your English Literature degree. For some students, who have followed English Language or English Language and Literature at A level, this will be a familiar ground. If, however, you studied English Literature only, it is likely to be new territory.

The possibility of following modules in English Language will of course depend upon your institution. Not all English departments will offer English Language, and you should check this out via the departmental web pages or prospectus. Where the possibility to undertake such study exists, the particular modules on offer will also vary from one institution to another, but typical areas for study are the following:

- the use and effects of language in literary texts;
- the sounds and structure of the English language;
- language and society;
- the historical development of the English language;
- the acquisition of language;
- language and politics;
- the structures of the English language;
- linguistic theory;
- sociolinguistics.

The purpose of studying language and linguistics is to understand how language works, how it changes over time and how it functions in social situations. Understanding in these areas can provide a stimulating alternative path within your studies of literature, and can also greatly enhance your engagement with the linguistic features of literary and non-literary texts.

MAIN ATTRIBUTES NEEDED TO SUCCEED IN AN ENGLISH LITERATURE DEGREE

Before committing yourself to applying for a degree in English Literature, it is very important to think about the characteristics you will need in order to succeed. There are, of course, no hard and fast answers to this, but here is a list of characteristics identified by English lecturers in higher education:

- communication skills;
- essay-writing skills;
- the ability to formulate, and sustain and develop an argument;
- analytical ability;
- dedication and self-motivation;
- note-taking and note-making abilities;
- independent study skills;

- interest and enthusiasm;
- research skills;
- intellectual curiosity;
- creativity;
- wide subject knowledge;
- knowledge of literary criticism and literary theory;
- wide reading;
- love of and confidence in reading.

It would be worth spending some time thinking about how far this list seems to relate to you, and also what you understand by each of these characteristics. If this sounds like you, and if the areas identified are areas in which you want to continue to develop, then English Literature may well be for you.

ACTIVITY 3

Your characteristics as a student

Think back carefully over your experiences as a learner:

- What have you done in the course of your study of English Literature to date (and at A level in particular) to prepare you in each of these areas?
- What have you done in your study of other subjects?
- How would you like to develop further in these areas?

APPLYING TO UNIVERSITIES

All applications to UK universities are made through UCAS. Much useful information and advice about the application process is available on their website: http://www.ucas.ac.uk/. The following sections provide a timeline of key dates in the application process, and guidance on writing Personal Statements and preparing for interviews.

APPLICATIONS TIMELINE

This timeline identifies on a month-by-month basis what should happen. For details about specific dates, please see the UCAS website.

September	Application processing begins.
October	Last date for applications to Oxford and Cambridge.
January	Deadline for applications from UK and EU students to be guaranteed equal academic consideration.
March	Universities and colleges should have sent decisions on all applications received by 15 January.
May	Applicants who have not responded to an offer made by 31 March will be automatically rejected.
	If universities have not made a decision on applications received by 15 January, these will be rejected by default.
June	Final deadline for receipt of applications for immediate consideration. Those received after this date held for Clearing.
July	If universities have not made a decision on applications received by 12 June, these will be rejected by default.
	Last date for applicants to refer themselves through Extra.
	Outstanding decisions on applications received by 30 June and Extra referrals rejected by default.
	Outstanding replies declined by default where last decision received by 20 July.
August	Publication of SQA results. Start of Scottish Clearing vacancy information service.
	All outstanding replies declined by default.
	Publication of GCE results.
	Start of English, Welsh and Northern Irish Clearing vacancy information service.
September	Last date for receipt of applications.

WRITING A PERSONAL STATEMENT

Lots of universities do not interview potential students, so your UCAS statement is extremely important. It is your opportunity to make a real impression on the Admissions Tutor reading your application. Remember that Admissions Tutors will probably be looking at hundreds of applications, as competition for places is heavy (especially on oversubscribed courses), so your Personal Statement needs to set you apart from other applicants.

Here are some of the key issues an Admissions Tutor is likely to be considering:

- are you suited to the course?
- are your qualifications and qualities right?
- are you conscientious and likely to complete the course?
- can you cope with the demands of the course?
- can you manage the workload?
- will you adjust to life and work at university?
- do you communicate effectively?
- have you researched the course well?
- do you demonstrate passion for your subject and desire to learn more about it?

Your Personal Statement does not need to address these issues mechanically, but you must demonstrate through a combination of statements about yourself and examples of what you have done to date, that you have the qualities required for the study of English at university (see pp. 10–11).

Do not try to write your statement straight out. Begin by jotting down notes about yourself and the course you are applying for. Also, look carefully at the web pages and prospectuses of the institutions you are applying for as well as any other information they may have sent you to see if they offer any particular guidance on how to present your Personal Statement. Here are some areas you could consider:

- what you want to study and why;
- particular areas of personal interest;

13

- good examples from your studies to date;
- your wider reading/writing;
- other subject experience;
- conferences you have attended (e.g. A-level literature lectures);
- personal experiences which led to your decision to apply;
- how a degree in English Literature relates to your future aspirations;
- your personal reliability, initiative and responsibility (e.g. employment, enterprise schemes, community/charity work, committee membership, assistance at school events, Young Enterprise, World Challenge, Duke of Edinburgh, participation in societies and what you have gained from these experiences);
- free time interests – for example sport, musical, study and leisure activities;
- languages which you speak;
- prizes won/positions achieved in your interests.

This should provide you with plenty of raw material for use in your Personal Statement. Remember that your primary objective is to show that you are enthusiastic about English Literature. You need to explain concisely how and why the subject appeals to you and that you have the personal qualities needed to succeed over the three years of your degree. Reading example Personal Statements (both good and bad) may well help you with this. Your school or college may well keep a stock of these.

As a rule of thumb, spend half of your statement talking about English Literature and why you want to study it, and spend the other half writing about yourself, your abilities and how these make you suitable to study the course. Where possible, these two components should be integrated with one another throughout the statement. You should develop a clear structure for your statement. This can be done in many ways, but make sure the structure you develop is clear and logical. Here is an example:

Paragraph 1: introduction to why you want to study English Literature.
Paragraphs 2 and 3: good examples of how you have studied the subject to date and how you would like to extend this.

Paragraph 4: work experience and responsibilities in school.
Paragraph 5: interests and responsibilities outside school.
Paragraph 6: your goals in going to university and closing comment.

Once you have gathered together your notes and thought about how you are going to structure your ideas, it is time to start writing. Remember the following:

- construct your statement carefully – you need to show you organise your ideas capably;
- express your ideas clearly and concisely – you must demonstrate you are a competent writer;
- make sure your writing is technically accurate – sloppy spelling, punctuation and grammar will turn an Applications Tutor off at once;
- this is a Personal Statement, so make sure your personality comes across;
- do not be arrogant and pretentious;
- make your opening and closing sentences tell;
- do not try to deceive – cheating yourself, other applicants and the Admissions Tutor will make nobody happy.

Remember you only have a limited amount of space, and so it is important to make every word count to be positive and interesting. Do not simply write about what you have done, but try to explain why you did it and what you learned from it. For example, 'I sat on the Sixth Form Committee, which taught me much about teamwork, responsibility and time management.'

Once you have completed the first draft of your statement, it is a good idea to put it aside for several days. This will help you develop some distance from it, so that when you return to it you will do so with a more critical eye. When you re-read it, make sure it reads well and is not confusing – if you are confused reading your own Personal Statement, you can be sure the Admissions Tutor will be too. Also, ask family, friends and teachers to read your statement and to make constructive comment. Consider carefully any advice you are given and develop your statement as you think is appropriate.

Advice on writing your Personal Statement can be found on the following websites. These offer structured guidance in thinking about the purpose and content of the Personal Statement.

http://www.ucas.com/students/startapplication/apply09/personal-statement/

http://www.studential.com/personalstatements/

http://www.getintouni.com/

There are also three books on writing Personal Statements:

- *Personal Statements: How to Write a UCAS Personal Statement* by Paul Telfer;
- *How to Write a Winning UCAS Personal Statement* by Ian Stannard;
- *How to Write a Successful University Personal Statement Application* by Matt Green and Ian Kingsbury.

PREPARING FOR AN INTERVIEW

It is comparatively rare for universities to interview applicants, but if a university calls you for an interview, you have done well in the first stage of your application. They like what they have seen on your UCAS form and they want to confirm that you are the right person for their course. They are interested in:

- you and your motivation;
- whether you are capable of studying at university level and completing the course successfully;
- your interest in the subject;
- what you will contribute to university life.

The interview is also an opportunity for you to confirm whether you like the university and want to study there. You will probably have the chance to see the campus and your department and may meet with current students. You should take the opportunity to ask any questions you have, to clarify any issues about course content and to follow up any queries you may have related to the prospectus.

The letter inviting you for interview should let you know what to expect on the day:

- will you have a general and/or subject interview;
- should you bring examples of your work;
- is some kind of written test involved;
- details of tours and meetings and so on.

If this is not all clear, you should ring the department and ask for this information.

In preparing for your interview, make sure you have read the university prospectus, departmental and generic web pages, and any other information the university has sent you thoroughly. This will help you to target your questions carefully and will avoid you asking questions to which a well-researched candidate will already know the answer. Also, make sure you plan out your journey thoroughly and arrive in plenty of time. It is better to arrive early and to spend two hours sitting in a coffee shop than to be panicking and chasing time. Arriving hot and flustered will not enhance your performance at interview, and reaching your appointment late will be viewed very badly by interviewers. If because of transport problems or for any other good reason you are delayed or cannot make your interview appointment, it is essential that you phone the university out of courtesy to let them know and to find out how to proceed. Contact details of the relevant person to contact should be on your offer of interview letter.

Think carefully about how you present yourself. Dress appropriately. Smart or smart casual clothing is most suitable. Make good eye contact with your interviewer, smile and respond appropriately when you are spoken to. Speak clearly and directly, as muttered answers are difficult to hear, and do not be afraid to ask for a little thinking time if you are asked a tricky question. Your interviewer will not mind, and taking a moment to formulate your thoughts so that you can give a coherent response is much better than launching at once into a rambling and inefficient answer. Ask sensible questions. In other words, make sure you appear confident (but not arrogant), interested and well prepared.

An important step in being well prepared for your interview is to think through likely questions and to shape your responses to them. This will give you confidence. Here are some typical questions you may face:

- *General questions*: Tell me about yourself? How would you describe yourself? Tell us about your current course? What are you best at? What are your main interests?
- *University motivation questions*: Why do you want to study for a degree? What do you think university can offer you? What else, apart from study, interests you about university? Why do you want to study at this university?
- *Subject-related questions*: Why do you want to study English Literature? What do you know about the course? What attracts you to this course? You may also be asked to complete an audit of your reading and to talk in detail about your study of a particular text, an area of literature you have studied (e.g. Gothic Fiction or Victorian Literature), or an unseen passage. Activities 1, 2 and 3 in this chapter will help you gather your thoughts in this area.
- *Topical questions*: interviewers often ask your opinion on current affairs, or subject-related issues in the media in order to see whether you are generally well informed and up to date. To prepare for this kind of question, read a serious national newspaper such as *The Times*, *The Telegraph* or *The Guardian*, pick out current stories that seem linked to your subject and think about how you could respond to a question on these topics.
- *Situational questions* (sometimes hypothetical): Give me an example of a time when...you dealt with a problem, or overcame some obstacles, or worked in a team to achieve an outcome. *Or* If you were asked to...do something creative about...what would you do?

Being well prepared to answer questions in these areas cannot guarantee success, and the types of question you are asked may vary, but if you spend time carefully thinking about things like this, you should go into your interview much more confident. And remember, you do not need to produce perfect instant answers. What you need to do is demonstrate that you are well prepared, well informed, well motivated and have the capacity to complete the course of study for which you have applied.

INDEPENDENCE

An important part of your experience at university is developing more independence. This obviously means changes in the ways you work. You will be expected to take much more responsibility for managing your own learning, and you will be expected to overcome difficulties using your own initiative. In course handbooks tutors will provide much useful information for you to look at which will help you answer your own problems. Reading lists will be supplied. Outline content of lectures and seminars will be provided. Specimen assessment materials may be included. There will probably be Virtual Learning Environments (VLEs) related to most of the modules you study as well as general departmental and university pages which will contain much of the information you need, and your tutors will expect you to familiarise yourself with these so that you can to a large extent help yourself. These resources will answer many of the logistical and academic questions you may have without having to go direct to the tutor.

You also have your peers on the course. They are another invaluable resource. The chances are that if you are having difficulty with a particular issue they are (or have done so) too.

Do not wait for tutors to check up on you. Most tutors will not, as a matter of course, make contact with the students on their courses. They will expect the initiative for contact to come from you. If you have a difficulty that you cannot sort out by any other means, do not wait for them to notice. The likelihood of this happening in a lecture you attend with a hundred other students is minimal. Equally, the chances for a tutor to follow up with individuals during or after seminars are often limited, and you will have to be the one who takes the initiative.

19

WORKING AT UNIVERSITY

It is very important to be creative in the ways you approach your work. A lot can be gained, for example, by thinking about how your peers can provide support. Students who make the time to meet regularly for study can do much to help each other in their work. While the opportunities to meet individually with staff are often limited at university, there is ample time available for you to run working groups and support groups of your own. With the exciting new independence studying at university offers, you need to develop proactive ways of meeting your own academic needs. The creation of alternative support structures – perhaps reading groups or informal student-led seminars – can be very helpful, if only to assure you that you are not alone. This is something you should think carefully about and can really help you to develop effective working practices. This will be explored fully in Chapter 3.

As you have already seen, lecturers will expect you to demonstrate a lot of independence. This level of freedom can seem intimidating, but can also be very liberating. Where during your A-level English Literature course did you really have the opportunity to explore a text widely without being forced back to think about Assessment Objectives? When did you have the chance to talk at length to other people in your class for hours over a coffee or a beer about varying interpretations of *Heart of Darkness?* Many aspects of studying English Literature are tied down at A level, which only allows you to study a narrow range of set texts. At university you have the exciting freedom to explore a much wider range of texts, and your independent study provides you with the time and space to pursue a far wider range of materials and ideas. Do not forget, you have come to university to 'read' for a degree. So take the chance to read as widely as you can and to make the time to talk to as many people as you can about your reading.

It has probably already begun to become clear that the teaching you receive at university is not and cannot be the main source of input into your studies. If you are taught for 9–12 hours per week – a typical teaching load in the first year of an English Literature degree – a lot of the responsibility obviously lies with you. You will soon get used to the jibes of students on other courses about how little you apparently have to do as a student of English:

> Q: Why don't English students look out of the window in the morning?
> A: Because if they did, they'd have nothing to do in the afternoon.

You, of course, will at this point adopt a superior attitude, treating the remark as the observation of a lesser form of pond life, take a long and pensive sip of your cappuccino, G&T or pint of mild, turn away, pick up your copy of *Pride and Prejudice* and immerse yourself once again in the world of Elizabeth Bennett and Mr Darcy. And whatever you do, take great care not to look out of the window.

More seriously, you will realise that your taught timetable accounts for only a comparatively small proportion of the time you should be studying. The time you spend in lectures and seminars represents only a third to a quarter of the time you should realistically be working. A lot of the responsibility for learning at university shifts on to you. Your lecturers will quite rightly consider themselves responsible for preparing and delivering appropriate teaching sessions, but you will bear a much greater level of responsibility for your own work than you probably did before. If you expect lecturers to provide you with all the answers, you will quickly be disillusioned. Lecturers do not see it as their job to provide answers. They will give you information, will present a variety of points of view and will raise many questions, but will not provide stock answers. They will see their lectures as the first word on a subject or text which you are then expected to go away and explore or challenge through your own independent studies.

Lectures and seminars, in other words, are a form of guidance. They indicate useful areas of study and salient ideas that can be brought to bear on a particular text, author or genre, which you as the student then have to pursue for yourself, with your lecturers' guidance. Some ways to prepare for seminars and lectures are covered in Chapters 4 and 5.

21

CONCLUSION

English Literature and the experience of studying it at A level, IB or Access level is very different from the experience of studying it at university. It is most important as you start your degree that you know two things which this chapter has hopefully helped you address:

- Where you are as you start your course – not geographically, of course, although this may prove to be invaluable knowledge in some ways. What do you already know about English Literature and where do you have gaps in your knowledge? How effectively do your characteristics as a student prepare you for working effectively at university?
- What has your study of the subject to date (at A level, IB or Access level) led you to believe the study of English Literature is about? What are you hoping to achieve through your studies?

As F. R. Leavis famously used to say, literature is where minds meet. In order effectively to meet others' minds it is important first to know your own.

2 Teaching and learning at university

By the end of this chapter you will have considered:

- how university courses are structured;
- how you will be taught at university;
- language and learning;
- types of modules;
- module selection;
- assessment of modules;
- breadth and depth of study at university;
- what learning styles are;
- what your own preferences in learning are;
- how learning styles relate to your study of English Literature.

INTRODUCTION

It is neither true nor helpful to say that A level does not prepare students for university. Yes, there are many ways in which sixth form and university English are different from each other, but with careful preparation, you can use your experiences of A level as an effective introduction to your university studies. Through studying English at A level, IB or Access you have already experienced and practised the majority of the skills you will need to succeed at university, it is just a case of thinking about how these experiences apply and need to be adapted.

Let us start by thinking about some of the main issues:

- there is an increased emphasis on independent study at university – some students fear this will make their studies a solitary and possibly isolating experience compared to the more 'shared' experience of learning within the sixth form environment;

- the study of English Literature at university is less prescriptive and more open in its nature – while A level tends to be heavily centred on a few set texts, university study of literature is much more holistic;
- after the teacher-led experience of A level, IB or Access courses, some students worry about the much more autonomous nature of university study;
- pace of study – the number of texts covered at degree level and the speed at which they are covered comes as a surprise to many students;
- some students mistake the nature of university study – university courses move quickly and cover a broad range of literature, but some students misunderstand this and see it as a sign of lack of depth;
- it is important to understand how you can use your independent study to provide depth of study – you need to think about how you will use your time to supplement and extend lectures, seminars and workshops;
- within the short contact time available on undergraduate courses, lecturers cannot cover everything and rely on you to take responsibility for your own learning.

It is important that as you approach your university studies you see teaching sessions in a different way. The roles and responsibilities of teachers and students in higher education are not the same as at A level, IB or Access. By careful thought, however, you can prepare yourself for the new challenges university study offers.

> I found the transition to degree level work hard. The pace and individual learning took some time to grasp.

It is important to take on board the implication that texts and issues covered in lectures, seminars and workshops need to be supplemented by detailed and extensive personal study. Here is what one university lecturer writes in the handbook for a first year Shakespeare module:

> The lecture is a way of introducing you to key concepts and ideas in relation to each of the texts studied, but it is a first rather than a last word on Shakespeare.

The onus is upon you to put into practice the principles and methods of literary study presented and modelled in lectures and seminars, a process with which your lecturers will help you.

HOW YOU WILL BE TAUGHT AT UNIVERSITY

Teaching and learning takes place in five main ways at university:

- *lectures* – these may vary in size, but will typically be delivered to large cohorts of students (often whole year groups); lectures will provide you with much information, but will offer little in the way of opportunities for interaction between the lecturer and the students;
- *seminars* – these are usually smaller in size, but may be groups of up to 30 students; seminars will provide information to supplement lectures, but will also provide the opportunity for structured discussion and activity;
- *workshops* – workshops are in some ways similar to seminars, but tend to be more creative and practical in their intentions; they will supplement lectures, and you will be expected to involve yourself actively in a range of activities;
- *tutorials* – these are increasingly rare, but you may receive tutorials either one-to-one or in a small group; these provide much more intensive opportunities to discuss your work;
- *independent study* – this underpins everything else that you do, and also draws it all together; you will be expected to spend substantial amounts of time each week in independent study, either individually or in small groups, as you arrange.

> Use teaching sessions as a springboard for developing your indepen-
> dent studies.
> *Lectures and seminars do not only impart information, they act as*
> *guides and help you build your own ideas and opinions.*

Full chapters are dedicated to lectures (Chapter 5), seminars and
workshops (Chapter 4) and independent study (Chapter 3) later in
this book.

THE BALANCE OF YOUR STUDIES

Balancing your studies at university is very important. It is very
easy to place far too much emphasis on lectures and seminars,
for example, and to misunderstand the importance of independent
study. Figure 2.1 demonstrates how the three major elements of

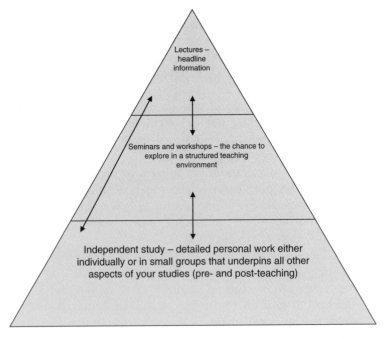

Figure 2.1 Aspects of your studies and how they relate to each other

your study of English Literature – lectures, seminars and independent study – relate to each other. It also shows the likely balance of time and importance in your studies. Lectures provide headline information and concepts, seminars provide a structured opportunity to explore these issues and independent study time is the bedrock on which successful participation in both lectures and seminars is founded.

LANGUAGE AND LEARNING

It is worth remembering that English as a subject is constructed around the four modalities of language: reading, writing, speaking and listening. All of these are an essential part of your experience of studying English Literature at university. F. R. Leavis used to say that Literature is where minds meet, and it is possible to understand your study of English Literature as a set of meetings. Figure 2.2 illustrates some of the kinds of 'meetings' that you will engage in as part of your studies. Language is obviously the central medium of these meetings, and it is therefore important to think carefully about the role the various modalities of language play in your studies.

ACTIVITY 4

Modalities of language

Think carefully about where each of these fits into your experience of study at university and respond to the following questions:

- Where will you write and what kinds of writing will you do?
- Where will you read, and what kinds of reading will you do?
- Where will you speak, with whom, and for what purposes?
- Where will you listen, to whom, and for what purposes?
- Look closely at Figure 2.2 – which of the modalities of language will you be using as you engage in these various 'meetings'?
- In what ways will these various 'meetings' take place in your studies?

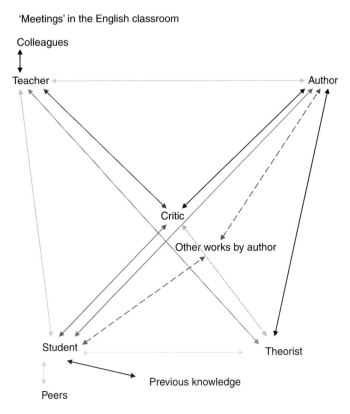

Figure 2.2 'Meetings' in the English classroom

HOW UNIVERSITY COURSES ARE STRUCTURED

Most courses at university now follow a modular structure. Modules carry credits at Level 1 (first year), Level 2 (usually second year) and Level 3 (usually third year). In order to attain your final degree you will have to achieve 360 credits: 120 at Level 1, Level 2 and Level 3. Modules are of two kinds: Compulsory (or Core) modules, which all students have to follow, and Option modules, which you will have the opportunity to select from a range of available options.

Year 1	Year 2	Year 3
120 Level 1 credits	120 Level 2 credits	120 Level 3 credits
360 credits – award of degree		

Depending on the quality of your performance in these different elements of your course, your university will – all being well – award you with your final degree. British universities award in the following bands:

- First Class;
- Upper Second Class;
- Lower Second Class;
- Third Class.

This may change to reflect the Burgess recommendations for the Higher Education Achievement Record (HEAR) – a move in the direction of something more like the US 'transcript'.

SELECTING MODULES

When it comes to selecting modules, it is important to think very carefully about the outcomes you want to achieve. These outcomes may be related to particular career aspirations and your plans for future study, either later in your degree or long term. Selecting modules should not be seen as a short-term activity, but needs to be seen in the long view. As is explained below, in order to follow some modules, certain choices have to be made early on (pre-requisites and co-requisites). Equally, some choices may preclude other choices. Look carefully at the module overview provided at Figure 2.4 to see examples of this.

WHAT TO LOOK FOR

Modules come in all shapes and sizes. Some will be compulsory, some will be optional. The possibility to study some modules will depend upon your having studied certain other modules first whilst

Compulsory modules	As their name makes clear, these are modules that all students on a particular degree programme have to follow. They are sometimes also known as **core modules**. These modules provide you with the major building blocks of your degree, and the learning you do through these will underpin work throughout your course. You should always look closely at how work undertaken in these modules relates out to the work you will do in your option modules.
Option modules	Again as their name makes clear, these are modules that you may choose to follow and which lie outside the core. For some of your degree, you are likely to have the opportunity to select what you want to study. Option modules will reflect the range of staff expertise and interest in your department and these can be very wide ranging. At various stages in your course you will be asked to make selections of the options you want to follow. Places on option modules cannot always be guaranteed, though, as class sizes often need to be limited because of staffing or rooming.
Pre-requisites	Sometimes you will see that modules have pre-requisites. This means that you cannot take this module unless you have already successfully completed the specified modules. You may not, for example, be allowed to take a Level 2 Shakespeare module without having first successfully completed the Level 1 module. This is because the content of the second module relies upon knowledge you will have gained in your study of the first module.
Co-requisites	Sometimes you will find that certain modules have what are called co-requisites. This means that modules must be taken in conjunction with each other. You may find, for example, that alongside a module in Romantic poetry you have to take a module in the rise of the novel. This is usually done to ensure you gain knowledge and understanding in related areas.
Electives	These are modules that may be open to you as part of your degree from other related programmes within the university (e.g. Creative Writing, Journalism, other Arts subjects, and even wider).

Figure 2.3 Modules – key terms

others will be free-standing. Some will relate to single authors (e.g. The Novels of Jane Austen), others will relate to groups of authors (e.g. Shakespeare and his Contemporaries). Some may relate to literary periods (e.g. nineteenth-century literature), others may relate to movements in literature (e.g. Modernism). Some may be 'short, fat' modules, taught over a single semester, others may be 'long, thin' modules taught over two semesters. You need to look carefully at the content and shape of modules when you are thinking about what you want to study and when you want to study it.

Figure 2.3 outlines some of the key terms you are likely to come across.

ACTIVITY 5

Module selection

Figure 2.4 is an example module overview for a degree course. Imagine you are a Single Honours student of English Literature.

Use this module overview to write down what your programme will be for the first year.

Remember the following:

- make sure you include all *compulsory* or *core* modules;
- take care not to select modules you are not allowed to follow;
- make sure you follow the rules about pre-requisites and co-requisites;
- remember that your programme must add up to 120 credits.

ASSESSMENT

Assessment at university in English Literature takes a variety of forms. Unlike at A level, where assessment tends to be quite narrowly defined according to Assessment Objectives, and where teachers frequently encourage students to see their progression in relation to these Assessment Objectives, assessment at university is of a rather different nature. Rather than thinking in terms of

Level 1, Semester 1	Level 1, Semester 2
AH1021 ACADEMIC PRACTICE 1 (20 credits) Compulsory for all Level 1 students in English	**AH1021 ACADEMIC PRACTICE 2 (20 credits)** Compulsory for all Level 1 students in English
EN1013 APPROACHES TO POETRY AND PROSE (20 credits) Compulsory for all Level 1 Single Hons. English students, Joint Hons. & Major-Minor English students must take *either* EN1014 *or* EN1013 *Not* available as an elective to non-English students	**EN1014 APPROACHES TO DRAMATIC TEXT (20 credits)** Compulsory for all Level 1 Single Hons. English students Joint Hons. & Major-Minor English students must take *either* EN1014 *or* EN1013 *Not* available as an elective to non-English students
EN1017 INTRODUCTION TO WRITING FICTION (20 credits) Compulsory for Creative Writing Students & English With Creative Writing Students Optional for Single Hons. English students & Joint Hons. & Major-Minor English students *Not* available as an elective to non-English students	**EN1015 THINKING ABOUT LITERATURE (20 credits)** Compulsory for all Level 1 students in English *Not* available as an elective to non-English students
EN1016 ENGLISH IN EVOLUTION (20 credits) Compulsory for Creative Writing Students *Not* available to English With Creative Writing Students, Single Hons. English students, Joint Hons. or Major-Minor English students *Not* available as an elective to non-English students	**EN1018 INTRODUCTION TO WRITING DRAMA (20 credits)** Compulsory for Creative Writing Students & English With Creative Writing Students *Not* available to Single Hons. English students Joint Hons. & Major-Minor English students *Not* available as an elective to non-English students
EN1002 MYTH AND ROMANCE (20 credits) Available as an elective to non-English students	**EN1000 EARLY MODERN WRITERS: SHAKESPEARE AND HIS CONTEMPORARIES (20 credits)** Available as an elective to non-English students

Figure 2.4 Example module overview

Assessment Objectives, lecturers will usually refer to the learning outcomes of study and you should make sure you are very clear about what these are, and you should think very carefully about how you can demonstrate your learning in these areas. The ways in which learning outcomes are expressed will vary from institution to institution, but Figure 2.5 provides an example from a second-year module on Romanticism and Revolution and a third-year module on Contemporary Writing.

Romanticism and Revolution

The module provides opportunities for students to develop and demonstrate knowledge and understanding, qualities, skills and other attributes in the following areas:

(A) Knowledge and Understanding

- Outline some of the connections between Romanticism and other literary and cultural movements of the eighteenth and nineteenth century.

(B) Cognitive (thinking) Skills

- Interpret particular Romantic works in relation to one another and to their social, political, philosophical, aesthetic and cultural contexts, deploying appropriate critical approaches.
- Show enterprise and selectivity in collecting and analysing evidence.

(C) Other Skills and Attributes (Practical/Professional/Transferable)

- Produce effective written communication and argumentation.

Contemporary Writing

The module provides opportunities for students to develop and demonstrate knowledge and understanding, qualities, skills and other attributes in the following areas:

(A) Knowledge and Understanding

1. Outline the variety of contemporary writing in English since 1980.
2. Relate the relationship between contemporary writing in English and its context(s): aesthetic, cultural, intellectual, social.

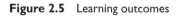

Figure 2.5 Learning outcomes

(B) Cognitive (thinking) Skills

1. Analyse the thematic interests and formal techniques used by a number of contemporary writers.
2. Explain and examine in detail the work of at least four contemporary writers covering the two literary genres of poetry and prose.

(C) Other Skills and Attributes (Practical/Professional/Transferable)

1. Independent study following up group-work.
2. Variety of material retrieval skills incorporating a number of media in a number of formats.

These learning outcomes have to be reflected in the form that actual module assessments takes. The nature of assessments will vary widely from one institution to another, but to illustrate, Figure 2.6 provides an example of a multi-stage assessment for a first-year course in Literary Theory:

There are five pieces of work for this course.

They are the following:

- Two essays of 1–1500 words with feedback during the course (each of these count for 20 per cent of the total course mark).
- One précis – A précis, of 500–1000 words, offers a detailed account of the argument of a section from *Literary Theory: An Introduction*. No more than 50 words from the original text are to be cited directly. The marks for this do not go towards the final mark for the course, but do count towards its completion.
- One seminar presentation – A seminar presentation during a seminar in the second semester. A presentation is a 10-minute response to the critical ideas that you are looking at that week. Notes on presentations are included below. The marks for this do not go towards the final mark for the course, but do count towards its completion.
- Two-hour exam (this counts for 60 per cent of the course mark).

Figure 2.6 Multi-stage assessment

This kind of staged assessment is common in university, where you will be working on modules over a semester and sometimes longer. Note also that in this kind of staged assessment some pieces of work are obligatory but do not form part of actual weighted assessment. The purpose of such assessed pieces is formative – designed to help you develop your own academic practices in English.

Assessment and how to approach assessment through your independent study is discussed in greater detail in Chapter 3.

BREADTH AND DEPTH OF STUDY

At A level, you probably studied eight or nine texts over the two years of your course. At university you will probably cover texts at the rate of one per week per module.

There is an important shift between the experience of studying English Literature at school or college and at university. At A level, IB or Access your study was probably based on a fairly small number of set texts. This will have covered the three major genres of poetry, prose fiction and drama. It may also have included some literary non-fiction, literary criticism and literary theory. Wider reading will also have comprised an element of your work. Still, however, the predominant method of working at this level will have been the in-depth study of a comparatively small number of texts. Wider reading will have provided you with some breadth, but teaching will have been focused on providing depth of knowledge.

At university the ratio is reversed. Teaching will be focused on covering a broad range, and your lecturers will expect you to use your independent study to provide the detailed in-depth study that needs to supplement their teaching. As you progress as a student of English Literature, as in any subject, you need to become more independent, and you should expect that much of the in-depth study of literature will be done by yourself or in small study groups you may set up.

At school we would look much closer at a text with a teacher. University asks you to look closer again, but by yourself. You need to learn how to juggle work more, prioritising work and so on as the work load is much heavier compared to A level.

PREPARING FOR INDIVIDUAL MODULES

Whenever you start a module at university it is always important to know where you are in terms of your knowledge. If you do not know where you are starting from, it is much more difficult to get to where you want to be. Figure 2.7 provides a useful model you may adopt for auditing what you know about the content of any given module you may be studying.

You can use this diagram as a template to audit your knowledge in certain areas of literature as you begin studying them, and then you can add to it as you progress. At the left-hand edge of the diagram you should identify texts or issues that you know very well. These may be literary or they may be contextual. You may, for example, have studied Victorian social and political history as

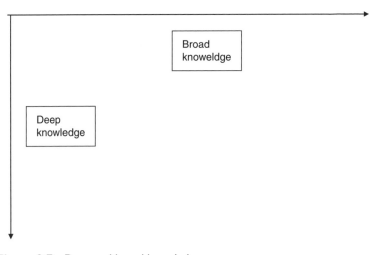

Figure 2.7   Deep and broad knowledge

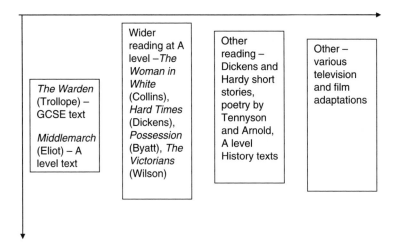

Figure 2.8 Victorian fiction

part of your History A level. This would be useful deep knowledge for a module looking at Victorian fiction. You can then use the rest of the diagram to indicate other areas of knowledge which are relevant. This may include texts you have read but not studied, other relevant reading, knowledge from other subject areas, television viewing and so on. Figure 2.8 provides an example taking the example of a module addressing Victorian fiction.

If you see that there are specific areas where you need to develop your subject knowledge in preparation for the study of a particular module, you can easily prepare for yourself a programme of initial reading to both broaden and deepen your knowledge. Figure 2.9 provides an example programme of reading you might undertake in preparation for the study of the First World War Literature.

Reading programme

- *Memoirs of an Infantry Officer* – Siegfried Sassoon
- *Scars on Their Heart* – an anthology of women's poetry from the First World War
- *Birdsong* – Sebastian Faulks

➤

Figure 2.9 The First World War literature

- *Strange Meeting* – Susan Hill
- *Regeneration Trilogy* – Pat Barker
- *A Testament to Youth* – Vera Brittain
- *All Quiet on the Western Front* – Erich Maria Remarque
- *A Farewell to Arms* – Ernest Hemingway
- *The Good Soldier Swejk* – Jaroslav Hasek
- *Three Soldiers* – John Dos Passos
- Follow this link for some German war poetry: http://www.worldwar1.com/sfgp1.htm and http://www.scuttlebuttsmallchow.com/listgerm.html
- Follow this link for French the First World War poetry: http://www.scuttlebuttsmallchow.com/listfren.html
- Follow this link for Russian poets: http://www.scuttlebuttsmallchow.com/listruss.html
- Follow this link for Austro-Hungarian poets: http://www.scuttlebuttsmallchow.com/listaust.html
- Follow this link for American poets: http://www.scuttlebuttsmallchow.com/listyank.html
- David Stevenson – *1914–1918: The History of the First World War* (Penguin Press, 2004).
- Benjamin Britten's *War Requiem* is a setting of the requiem mass alongside setting of Owen's poetry. Sir Arthur Bliss also wrote a major piece called *Morning Heroes*. Cyril Rootham wrote *For the Fallen*.
- Ivor Gurney was both a poet and a composer who produced some interesting work in both fields.
- Look at some of the major artists of the First World War (a good selection of artists from a range of national backgrounds can be found following this link: http://www.art-ww1.com/gb/peintre.html#)
- Look at the First World War photography – good selections at http://www.gwpda.org/photos/greatwar.htm and http://www.firstworldwar.com/photos/index.htm

WHAT KIND OF LEARNER ARE YOU?

It is important to think not only about what you are going to learn, but also about how you learn. A number of educational theorists

Intelligence type	Capability and perception
Linguistic	Words and language
Logical-mathematical	Logic and numbers
Musical	Music, sound, rhythm
Bodily-kinaesthetic	Body movement control
Spatial-visual	Images and space
Interpersonal	Other people's feelings
Intrapersonal	Self-awareness

Figure 2.10 Gardner's Multiple Intelligences

have put forward models of what are called learning styles. Probably the best known of these is the model by Howard Gardner. He identifies a range of styles by which people learn, summarised in Figure 2.10:

ACTIVITY 6

Learning styles

Think carefully about each of these styles of learning. How does each of them relate to the study of English Literature? They all do in some ways – even the one about numbers! How could you create opportunities to use each of these learning styles within your independent study? Which are you most likely to use in lectures? Which will you use in seminars? How can you develop your abilities in each of these styles of learning? What will each add to your experience of studying English Literature?

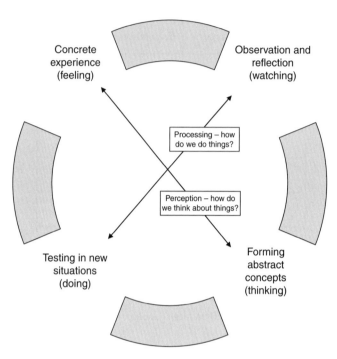

Figure 2.11 Kolb's Learning Cycle

Another theorist, David Kolb, puts forward another model, summarised in Figure 2.11:

Kolb envisages learning as a cycle beginning with experience and then working sequentially through observation and reflection through abstract conceptualisation to testing which, in its turn, leads back to new concrete experience. These four stages operate in pairs – experience and abstraction are related to cognitive processes or thinking, while observation and testing are related to action.

ACTIVITY 7

Learning cycle

Look carefully at Kolb's Learning Cycle. How does this help you to think about your role in university learning. Try to relate each of the four stages Kolb identifies to lectures, seminars or workshops and independent study. Where does each seem to fit? How does this help you understand more about your role in the process of teaching and learning?

CONCLUSIONS

The experience of teaching and learning at university is very different from the experience of teaching and learning at A level, IB or Access. It is important that you make yourself familiar with the new demands of your particular department as soon as you can. Remember, all that you have learned through A level, IB or Access is directly relevant to what you will be studying at university and also to how you will be studying it. You do need to spend time (sometimes substantial amounts of it) working out how your experience of English Literature to date relates to what you will be doing at university. Thinking reflectively about both what you have learned and how you have learned it is an essential starting point.

3 Independent study

By the end of this chapter you will have considered:

- what your lecturers will expect of independent study;
- how independent study at university differs from independent study at A level, IB or Access;
- how to organise your week, including preparing a study plan;
- how to prepare for lectures and seminars;
- how to prepare for assignments;
- studying alone;
- studying in pairs;
- studying in larger groups;
- how to use module handbooks;
- using the library.

INTRODUCTION

As you are taught less at university, it should come as no surprise that you will need to spend longer than you used to on independent study. But how long should you spend? The answer to that question will depend on how many taught hours your weekly programme consists of. Your tutors may well give you guidance on this. As a rule of thumb, however, you should reckon to spend around 35 hours per week on your studies. Your degree is, after all, your employment for the next three years.

How you distribute this time is, of course, up to you. Some of you may choose to work 'office hours' – nine to five, Monday to Friday. Many of you, however, will be balancing the demands of academic work with the requirements of paid employment and/or your family. The key issue is not how you arrange your independent study time, but that you allow yourself sufficient time to do the independent work you need to in order to enjoy and succeed in your studies.

Let us assume that you have a taught timetable of nine hours per week in the first year. That means you should be spending about 25 hours per week on independent study. This may sound a long a lonely occupation, but it need not be so. There is no reason why independent study needs to be an isolating experience. The keys to success are organisation and imagination. Some of your time must be spent alone with your own thoughts, but you should also arrange to work in pairs and groups. This can be very useful and rewarding.

FREEDOM – A BLESSING OR A CURSE?

> The thing that I have found most difficult, academically, about the move to university is the independence one receives. In contrast to school, it is up to the individual to hand work in, attend seminars and lectures and to do background reading and so on. This has been particularly difficult as it is not something I was used to at school. Coming from a high achieving school, where the focus was strongly on academics, and work would be chased up, lessons missed had to be explained and research was monitored, this has been particularly difficult for me.

For many students university offers a world of freedom that they have not experienced before. Large amounts of non-contact time will be a regular feature of your days, and it is all too tempting to see this as free time. Tutors will not apply the kinds of pressure to work that you have probably experienced before, nor will they offer the kinds of support you are probably used to. They will not chase you to submit work and meet deadlines. They will expect you to take responsibility for your own study. So, it is essential that you carefully organise yourself to ensure that you complete work effectively. Structuring your working week – including time for social activities – is essential, and will make your studies and your leisure time more fulfilling and enjoyable.

Lack of organisation when it comes to independent study is a repeated theme amongst students. It would be a shame if you allow this to happen to you. Independent study can be one of the most fulfilling and exciting parts of your degree, but without careful planning it can become one long round of chasing your tail.

In order to make your independent study efficient and enjoyable, it is worth arranging a personal weekly study timetable. Your department should provide you with guidelines about how much time you should spend studying independently. This is essential information, as it indicates how much work your lecturers think you should be doing to prepare for and to follow up on lectures and seminars. If you are spending considerably more or considerably less time than this, you need to ask yourself why. If you do not receive guidance on this important point, ask the departmental office, your lecturers or your personal tutor who should all be able to help you. Or use the advice offered in this chapter to help.

ACTIVITY 8

Independent study activity

Think carefully about the following questions:

- How much independent study were you expected to do when you were doing your A Levels?
- What did you spend your study time doing?
- How did you prepare for/follow up on your lessons?
- Where is the best place for you to study?
- Do you like studying alone or do you prefer working in small study groups?
- What are the advantages/disadvantages of each?

THE STUDY CYCLE

You may well find it useful to think of your study not as one large activity, but rather to see it as a set of three related stages. These stages are all related to teaching sessions (lectures or seminars, and occasionally workshops or tutorials), which are taken as the centre – although not necessarily the most important part – of the process. These stages will be used throughout this book to try to help you organise your thoughts about studying:

(1) *Pre-teaching (Preparation)*: this is all the preparatory work you will do prior to a module or teaching session. It will include reading of a variety of texts, note-making (different from note-taking, which happens in lectures), writing, discussion, thinking. All of these things will be done to prepare you for the central teaching session(s) so that you can actively participate. There is no reason for you ever to be passive, even in a lecture, as long as you have prepared yourself effectively.

(2) *During teaching (Delivery)*: this covers your role in teaching sessions. These are the things you should do in order to make the experience of the lecture or seminar in question as enjoyable and as profitable as possible in terms of learning for you and all the other members of your group. It will involve participation, thinking, note-taking, writing, reading, showing respect. It also involves ensuring that you have an effective record of the session so that you can use it in subsequent lectures and seminars and in your independent studies.

(3) *Post-teaching (Evaluation)*: this is the way(s) in which you follow up on teaching sessions in your independent study, either as a record for assessments and examinations, or to prepare for future work. It involves writing up notes, undertaking further reading and research, and perhaps rereading. It also involves thinking about how effectively you prepared for these teaching sessions and considering whether you need to develop your working practices.

It is important to see your studies as a cycle. If you follow the preparation, delivery, evaluation model suggested above this will help you to make more confident and constructive progress through your degree. It will ensure that you are always looking both backwards and forwards through your studies, which will allow previous learning to inform new learning, and will also allow new learning to help with the revision and challenging of previous learning. This way your learning will become a dynamic process.

The study cycle

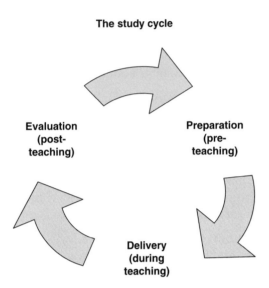

**Evaluation
(post-
teaching)**

**Preparation
(pre-
teaching)**

**Delivery
(during
teaching)**

YOUR TIMETABLE

One of the most important issues you will face as you begin your
course is your teaching timetable. The first thing you will probably
notice is the acres of non-contact time that you have. Although
you will receive more English teaching, the overall amount of time
you spend in the classroom will decrease. This may well come as
a surprise. Lots of students anticipate more teaching at university
than they receive. Most English students are in the classroom for
between six and ten hours a week.

It is obviously important to think about how this will affect you.
Clearly it means making significant changes to your working pat-
terns. In the sixth form or at college, you were probably in classes
for between 18 and 24 hours per week in total. Yes, you were
expected to do fairly extensive independent study as well, but the
majority of your work was probably undertaken in the classroom.
That will change at university, where you are expected to direct
your own studies for the majority of your time. What you study,
when you study it and the ways in which you set about your

learning are much more under your own control. This is both the biggest challenge and the most exciting part of studying English at university.

CONTACT WITH ACADEMIC STAFF

Your relationship with staff is also likely to be different. At A level you were probably taught in small groups, whereas lectures and seminars are often delivered to much larger groups, where your relationship with lecturers and peers is likely to be rather different. These changes provide all kinds of exciting opportunities for you as you develop as a student of English, but will require you to make some big changes in the ways you work and think and you will need to develop a range of new ways of managing your learning. We will think about this more in Chapters 4 and 5, which deal with seminars and lectures, respectively.

It is important to be aware that your contact with academic staff at university will probably be regulated in ways that contact with staff at school or college is not. Tutors frequently operate systems of office hours. This is an allotted period in the week at which students can make appointments to discuss work with them. Obviously the number of students tutors can see within these hours is limited, so it is important to make yourself aware of these office hours and to book early if you wish to make an appointment. You can always contact lecturers via email, but it is worth remembering that just because an email is delivered, it does not mean a reply will come immediately. Your lecturers are busy people, and most do not come into university every day, as they will be undertaking preparation, research and writing. When they are in university they also have other responsibilities, such as management roles and assessment. They also often teach on a variety of courses, and so will not always be available. Alternatively, lecturers frequently attend conferences and may not pick up emails at once. This means that you need to think carefully about whether you really need to contact a member of staff and how you choose to contact them. The possibility for you to raise concerns or questions directly with members of teaching staff is more limited than you may be used to.

ORGANISING YOUR TIME

> When you come to university you're supposed to be more independent and able to motivate yourself and focus yourself, so I suppose that if they did give us a list of everything we had to think about and a list of tasks and things, we'd never ever really be prepared at all for anything unless we had a list of instructions.

The following section offers some useful suggestions about how you can organise your time and create a structured framework for your studies.

PREPARING A WEEKLY STUDY TIMETABLE

A very good place to start is to prepare a weekly study plan. Maybe you already have your teaching timetable, maybe you are waiting for it, or perhaps you are already part way through your first year. Whatever your situation, this exercise will help you to find a way of managing your study that works for you.

For the purposes of the exercise, you are to assume you have a nine-hour weekly taught programme. You are following four modules on:

- Shakespeare;
- Poetry;
- the Novel; and
- Medieval Literature.

Each of these modules has two timetabled hours per week (one lecture and one seminar). In addition you have a weekly session on academic writing which lasts for one hour.

Plan a weekly study timetable on the basis that you will work nine to five, Monday to Friday, as this will be the easiest to manage at first. Bear in mind the following principles, all of which you should incorporate in your study programme:

- make planned time for reading key primary texts ahead of lectures and seminars;
- make planned time for doing secondary reading ahead of lectures and seminars;
- allow time for revisiting and completing notes after lectures and seminars (ideally on the same day, but certainly as soon as possible after the lecture is over);
- make time for discussing your reading and the content of lectures and seminars with your peers;
- block out a regular slot of extended time for the preparation and writing of assignments.

Use a simple template like the one at Figure 3.1 to help you. The times of lectures and seminars are already written in.

	Monday	Tuesday	Wednesday	Thursday	Friday
9–10					
10–11		Poetry lecture			Novel lecture
11–12		Poetry seminar	Shakespeare lecture		
12–1	Lunch	Lunch	Lunch	Lunch	Lunch
1–2			Shakespeare seminar		Novel seminar
2–3	Medieval Lit. lecture				
3–4	Medieval Lit. seminar			Academic writing class	
4–5					

Figure 3.1 Study timetable template

	Monday	Tuesday	Wednesday	Thursday	Friday
9–10	Read play for Shakespeare lecture on Wednesday	Theory reading for Friday's Novel lecture	Library – journal reading for Shakespeare lecture	Assignment preparation and writing	Peer study group – Novel (see p.54)
10–11		Poetry lecture			Novel lecture
11–12		Poetry seminar	Shakespeare lecture		Theory reading for Tuesday's poetry lecture
12–1	Lunch	Lunch	Lunch	Lunch	Lunch
1–2	Re-read poems and prepare for Poetry lecture and seminar	Finish Poetry lecture and seminar notes – paired work	Shakespeare seminar		Novel seminar
2–3	Medieval Lit. lecture		Finish Shakespeare lecture and seminar notes – small group	Assignment preparation and writing	Finish Novel lecture and seminar notes
3–4	Medieval Lit. seminar	Begin reading novel for Friday's lecture and seminar		Academic writing class	Reading and translation for Monday's Medieval Lit. lecture
4–5	Finish Medieval Lit. lecture and seminar notes		Complete reading novel for Friday's lecture and seminar	Read poems for Tuesday's Poetry lecture and seminar	

Figure 3.2 Example completed study timetable

Figure 3.2 shows a suggested completed version, adopting all the principles suggested above.

Note that this timetable deals with at least two modules each day. This serves a number of purposes. First, it provides variety. To spend all day working on the same material can be frustrating, and this is unproductive. Moving from one topic or module to another provides a welcome change and helps to keep your mind fresh. But it serves other purposes too. The study of English Literature at university is less about the study of set texts (which tends to be the primary focus of A Level and IB) and more about developing your broader abilities as a student of literature. By ensuring that you cover more than one topic or module per day in your independent study, you will begin to discover connections. You will see how theoretical readings of one text apply to others, and you will develop a growing sense of how literary periods and genres compare and contrast with one another.

You will also notice that even amounts of time have not been allowed for all modules. This is not to imply that certain modules are more important than others, or that some courses carry more weight in assessment than others (although you should always check the credit-weighting of assessment for modules carefully). Here the differing amounts of time allotted reflect the practical reading demands attached to each module. The novel module, for example, is allowed ten hours to reflect the practical issues of reading what will certainly be a substantial (possibly a very substantial) text. The Shakespeare module is given eight hours. Most Shakespeare plays can realistically be read at a single sitting within two to three hours, including note-making, so less time has been granted. The poetry module and medieval literature module are allowed six and five hours, respectively. This is because reading here tends to be of shorter texts, although this may not necessarily be the case. If, for example, the poetry course is addressing large-scale poetic works such as Spenser's *Faerie Queene*, Milton's *Paradise Lost* or some of the major poems of the Romantics, like Byron's *Childe Harold*, Shelley's *Prometheus Bound* or Blake's prophetic books, then longer time periods for reading may be required.

Two further points to consider are the following:

- how far in advance should you be preparing for teaching? – clearly you should not leave this too much to the last minute, as rushed preparations are rarely adequate preparations. You need to leave yourself an appropriate amount of time in which to complete what needs to be done. To do your preparatory study too far in advance, however, is also unhelpful, as you need your preparatory work to be fresh in your memory. As with so many things in your studies, striking a good balance is important;
- think regularly about whether your timetable is meeting your needs – as modules develop and as you become aware of your

needs, revisit your timetable to make sure it is appropriate, and change it if it is not. You may also wish to change your timetable for variety.

ADAPTING YOUR TIMETABLE

When it comes to devising your study timetable there are no hard and fast rules. The amounts of time you will need to spend on different parts of your studies will vary according to a range of factors, including how quickly you read, the accessibility of library resources, time to travel across campus or between campuses and so on. In reality you may not wish to or be able to organise your work on a nine-to-five basis. You may prefer to work shorter days during the week and include time for study at weekends. Or you may need to arrange your study differently to allow for paid employment. If this is the case, devise a more suitable programme for yourself. The most important thing is that you do devise a regular study plan. By developing such a study timetable you will efficiently take control of your studies, rather than allowing them to run away with you.

To make sure that your study timetable is working efficiently, you should revisit it from time to time and make any necessary adjustments. Your timetable should be flexible to take into account the changing demands of your studies. If, for example, you are following a module on the Victorian novel and have to prepare long novels by Dickens, Collins, Trollope and George Eliot, you will have to allow more time for reading. Or if you are giving a seminar presentation you will need to prepare and may need to meet up with other students. Eventualities like this have to be overcome, but they are always more easily managed when you have developed an efficient study programme in the first place.

SUMMING UP

A good study timetable will:

- make you an efficient manager of your work;
- be adaptable to meet the changing demands of your course;

- reflect your needs, including eating, sleeping and socialising;
- prevent you from aimlessly wading through the many and diverse requirements of your course;
- help you to keep on track with reading of both primary and secondary texts;
- help you prepare for lectures and seminars and follow up on them effectively;
- keep you moving meaningfully towards the completion of written and other assessment tasks.

STUDYING ALONE

Individual study is an important part of university life. Although lectures, seminars and discussions with other students are all important, it is essential that you make regular and sustained times when you can reflect personally on what you have learned. Reading, of course, will also largely be undertaken on an individual basis both before and after lectures and seminars, but this is covered in depth later on.

Here are some of the major purposes of individual study:

- to prepare for lectures, seminars and tutorials;
- to reflect on the content of lectures, seminars, tutorials and discussions with peers;
- to prepare for and complete assignments and assessments of varying kinds.

Let us think about each of these purposes in turn.

PREPARING FOR LECTURES, SEMINARS AND TUTORIALS

It is no good turning up for lectures, seminars or tutorials unprepared. It is important that you are organised in advance and that you take time on your own to prepare for them. First you should ensure that you have undertaken all relevant reading. This will include the text or texts the lecture is about and also a range of relevant secondary reading, which your lecturer or seminar leader will suggest. You should also make sure that you have spent time to formulate your own thoughts about the text and any particular focuses the lecturer or seminar leader has identified.

Most lecturers provide module handbooks. These are an essential source of information. They generally include information about:

- the objectives and outcomes of the module;
- where and when teaching takes place;
- expectations of students;
- primary texts covered;
- essential and recommended secondary reading;
- details about assessment.

They also usually tell you on a week-by-week basis what will be covered in lectures and seminars. The following are typical issues they will identify:

- key points of lecture;
- key issues for discussion;
- major themes;
- important theoretical perspectives and so on.

Here is an example from a first year Shakespeare module hand-book. First let us look at the overall rationales of the module (see Figure 3.3). These are clearly stated at the beginning of the handbook:

ACTIVITY 9

Thinking about modules

- Write down what you think are the main aims and purposes of this Shakespeare module.
- Also jot down the kinds of questions this is prompting you to ask about Shakespeare and his plays.
- How does this differ from the kinds of work on Shakespeare you have done up until now?

This course will introduce you to the close study of a wide range of Shakespeare's plays. The objective of the course is to facilitate a deeper – as well as a more pleasurable and rewarding – understanding of the range of Shakespeare's work. The course is broadly chronological. In this first semester we will concentrate on the genres of comedy and history, before going on to study the tragedies and romances next semester. As the course progresses, you will be encouraged to think about the plays as theatre as well as printed literature; but a main feature of the course will be its close attention to the extraordinary fertility and force of Shakespeare's dramatic language. While paying some attention to Shakespeare's very different historical context in the Renaissance, we will be equally concerned with the question of whether the plays are still relevant to us today. By the end of the course, you should have developed a good working knowledge of Shakespeare's dramatic and literary craft and be able to think and write intelligently, confidently and creatively about the plays.

Figure 3.3 Module rationale

It seems that the course leader particularly emphasises four issues:

- the plays as theatre and as text;
- the genres Shakespeare employs;
- use of language;
- historical-cultural context both at the time of the plays' composition and today.

ACTIVITY 10

Thinking about Shakespeare

Think carefully about these four issues

- Which of these issues has your study of Shakespeare to date prepared you effectively to do?
- Which has it not prepared you to do?
- What things might you do to address these?

55

REFLECTING ON LECTURES, SEMINARS, TUTORIALS AND DISCUSSIONS WITH PEERS

Your engagement with lectures and seminars does not end once the session is over. Hopefully you will come out of your teaching sessions with a stimulating set of notes and ideas. These now need further thought and research. As we saw earlier, lectures and seminars are intended to provide the first, not the last word on the text or topic you are studying. So it is important to revisit and develop the notes you have made during lectures and seminars. Ideally this should happen as soon as possible after the teaching session has finished, so that your recollections are as full and fresh as possible. When you go back to your session notes you should aim to convert them into:

- a set of more detailed and developed notes, which expand on and refine the notes you took during the teaching session. These notes will provide the basis for written assignments, will be needed to revise for examinations and may also provide useful background information for modules followed later in your course and even beyond;
- a plan for following up and researching key ideas. This may mean trips to the library, discussions with your peers, emailing or making an appointment with your lecturer or seminar leader.

Look again at the example study timetable (Figure 3.2). Note that time is set aside for this process on each day when lectures and seminars occur. This is well worth adopting as a principle. It will ensure that you remain on top of your notes and develop personal responses to what you are learning. This is particularly important at university where a wide range of texts and issues are often covered at high speed, and where you will be following a number of modules simultaneously. Regularly revisiting your notes will also help you to maintain a sense of how your understanding and ideas have developed through modules. Layers of understanding and detail are unlikely to be appreciated fully in the course of a single lecture, but are more likely to be the outcome of sustained periods of study throughout a module or sequence of modules.

PREPARING FOR ASSIGNMENTS

Arrangements for assessment and the ways in which this is undertaken can vary considerably from institution to institution. You may be assessed individually in groups, orally and/or in writing, by means of web-based or ICT assessments, through creative responses to text, or in a range of other ways. You should be made aware early in any module what form your assessment will take and when submission is due. It is worth noting the following general points about assessment in English Literature at university, however:

- the majority of assessment still takes place by writing essays;
- sometimes there will be another form of assessment employed as well, but often this will be a minority part of the assessment – always, therefore, look carefully at what proportion of the overall assessment for a module depends upon the element you are completing, so that you do not spend too long on something that is worth only a minority of the marks for a module or vice versa;
- sometimes modules will include compulsory tasks or activities (e.g. presentations, writing synopses, workshop writing) that are not credit rated in assessment – usually failure to complete these activities will lead to a penalty deduction from final assessment, however.

Assignments come in all shapes and sizes, and so it is impossible to provide examples of exactly the type of assignment you will be set. It is worth looking at an example, though. This is taken from a first-year module handbook, this time a module on Epic. This module covers texts from a range of periods and cultures. It focuses on the generic issues common to the texts covered, including Homer's *Iliad*, Virgil's *Aeneid*, Milton's *Paradise Lost*, Pope's *Rape of the Lock*, Keats' *Hyperion* and *The Fall of Hyperion*, Eliot's *The Waste Land*, and Walcott's *Omeros*.

The means by which the module will be assessed are clearly identified:

Method of Assessment

Essay and context questions. Each student will write one essay, to be taken from the past examination paper appended at the end of this course book. This essay will be no more than 2000 words, and must be submitted *by the first day after reading week, no later than 4.00 p.m.* Extensions to the essay deadline *must be negotiated in advance*, and will only be given for genuine cases.

Examination will be by two-hour sat paper. The exam will be in two sections, and will include (A) a selection of passages from syllabus texts, three of which are to be identified, placed in context and discussed for any features of interest (20 minutes for each), and (B) an essay question (one hour). Last year's exam paper is included at the end of this booklet.

The coursework assessment for this module offers a choice of over 20 questions. Although you will no doubt be used to having a choice of titles in both coursework and examinations, such a wide range of choice is probably something new to you. The range of questions on offer makes it more likely that you will find a question to which you are happy to respond. However, wide choice poses its own difficulties. There may, for example, be several questions you would like to answer, and you have to make the selection of just one. How do you demonstrate your understanding of a complex genre by answering only one task? How do you demonstrate your knowledge of a wide range of literary and theoretical material within 2000 words?

It is important to understand the long-term approaches to assessment adopted at university. Assessment tasks will probably be available to you from early in the module, when you receive your handbook. Preparation, research and writing of the assignment should, therefore, be undertaken not in the immediate run-up to the hand-in date, but over the course of the module. It is clear from the examination brief that you would be expected to know at least three of the core texts for the module in detail in order to respond to the context questions. Such knowledge can only be attained through systematic and sustained study, which is the great pleasure of reading for an English Literature degree. As demonstrated in the example timetable in Figure 3.2, regular weekly time should be allotted to the preparation and completion of assessments. Adopting such a long-term view of assessments will:

- help you make appropriate selection of task(s);
- ensure adequate preparatory reading in both primary and secondary texts;
- allow you to consider how wider issues relating to the module and other texts can be incorporated within the final assignment;
- ensure you have time to look at exemplar questions and understand the rubric for assessment.

Armed with this information, you should devise for yourself a schedule to prepare for and complete assessments, whatever form they take. From very early in a module you will be able to undertake meaningful preparation for end-of-module assessments. This may be done by:

- developing structured programmes of primary and secondary research;
- making notes;
- doing exploratory pieces of writing in response to key issues and texts;
- drafting material for inclusion in the final assessment and so on.

Even where assessment is by means of a sequence of shorter assignments throughout a module or semester, you should devise structured and sustained programmes of theoretical reading, evidence gathering and note-making that will progressively inform your responses and will help you to develop through the course of the module. By engaging in this type of preparatory work over a sustained period, you will ensure that:

- you have undertaken extensive and structured preparatory reading – your assignment will be well researched;

- where you are required to make a selection from a list of assessment options, you have time to make an appropriate choice;
- you will have ample time to clarify difficulties or queries about the structure and nature of the assessment with your lecturers;
- you will be confident that you are progressing towards the completion of the assignment, rather than rushing to complete work as a deadline looms;
- you will be able to develop and refine your ideas, your arguments and the evidence you employ over time, rather than having to form these hurriedly and without due consideration at the last minute;
- you will have time to present and reference your assignment correctly, in accordance with departmental or institutional guidelines.

By working this way you will avoid the stress that arises when you leave assignments until close to deadlines. It will also enable you to use lectures and seminars as a means of exploring ideas you may wish to use in your assignments, and to question lecturers or seminar leaders on these issues. These advantages may be lost if you leave the preparation and completion of assignments until the last minute.

PEER GROUP STUDY

Whilst a lot of your work will inevitably be undertaken individually for practical reasons, studying in pairs can be very useful. Learning is a social activity, and talk is an important part of the process. Talking about literature with other students on your course is one of the most pleasurable aspects of your studies, and you should not underestimate the value of simply sitting and talking about books. Whether in a structured or an unstructured environment (and you should make sure that you make the most of both) discussing your reading will develop your confidence to talk about literature and will enable you to become more and more familiar with the ideological and theoretical world of English

Literature. Talking improves thinking and well-directed talking improves thinking even more.

The opportunity to meet with your peers and to discuss your work is therefore very important for a number of reasons:

- it allows you to share your views and opinions about texts in a less formal environment than lectures and seminars;
- it helps you to work through personal difficulties, likes and dislikes with the texts or authors you are studying – another person's perspective is often very helpful in this process;
- it provides the space and time for you to clarify some of the complex ideas and theoretical issues you will come into contact with – sometimes these can be effectively worked through alone, but again the views of another person can be very helpful here;
- it helps you to develop confidence in discussing primary and secondary texts – this is likely to improve your ability to make effective contributions in lectures and seminars;
- it can be good to discuss the content of lectures and seminars, both before and after they occur – this way you can be well prepared for involvement and will not simply have to react (or more often not react) to what happens in the teaching session;
- it is a good forum for sharing useful information about reading, useful texts for comparison.

STUDYING IN PAIRS

Before we begin thinking about the advantages of studying in pairs, it is worth spending a moment considering your choice of study partner. You will be spending a lot of time working closely with them, and so this is an important decision. The following are all important things to think about:

- How many different people do you want to work with? There is no reason why your partner should be the same for all modules (in fact to gain a range of different experiences, it might be advisable to seek variety);

- Is this person reliable? This is very important, because otherwise your study sessions may be unprofitable or may not happen at all;
- Is the person a willing contributor? You need to be sure that you will gain from as well as give to the partnership;
- Do you tend to agree or disagree with this person? Sometimes it is important and stimulating to have your views challenged;
- Is the person well organised? You will be relying on your partner to undertake certain activities, and you need to know they will be organised in undertaking them.

Once you have selected your study partner you then need to agree carefully what it is that you are both hoping to achieve through your paired study. It is well worthwhile having an initial meeting where you discuss this in detail. If you are both pursuing different agendas then your meetings may become frustrating. Of course you must be flexible, and your ideas may change over time, but it is far more likely that your work together will be profitable and happy if a few essential ground rules are in place. You might also think about discussing your paired study with your lecturers. They may well be able to suggest issues and materials that would be useful for you to consider during your meetings, and they may be able to find ways of incorporating this in their lectures and seminars.

Obviously it is important that you prepare individually before paired study sessions. It is also useful to agree beforehand what you will each look at in order to avoid duplication and to make sure that you use of your time constructively. If you do not do this, your discussions will tend to lack focus and direction. In addition it is important that prior to the meeting you have agreed upon the issues to be discussed and how you will prepare for it. Here are a few useful questions to consider:

- Will you base your discussion solely on primary texts (e.g. *A Tale of Two Cities* or *Waiting for Godot*)?
- Will your discussion focus on both primary and secondary texts (e.g. the plays of John Marston and T. S. Eliot's essay on Marston as dramatist)?

- Will you discuss theoretical texts only, relating the ideas you find in them freely to your reading and work for the full range of modules you are following?
- Will you both read the same pre-arranged secondary text(s) and explore the issues they raise in relation to the primary text you are considering?
- Will you both read different secondary texts and, through debate, argue the relative merits of each as a perspective from which the primary text may be read?

There are no right and wrong answers to these questions. Variety, as they say, is the spice of life, and you will quite rightly want to experiment with what you do in paired study sessions. There is one hard and fast rule, however, if these study sessions are to be successful. You need to sit down with your partner and make decisions which are agreeable to you both. This should be done in advance of the paired study session with suitable time allowed to do any necessary preparation. Without this, you cannot make the best use of your time together. Also think clearly about what outcomes you want from the shared study session. These may be of various kinds:

- to develop an introductory set of notes prior to a lecture or seminar;
- to draw up a list of questions to ask your lecturer or seminar leader;
- to prepare for an assignment;
- to deepen your understanding of new concepts;
- to share 'discoveries' from your personal reading;
- to develop a framework for note-taking for use within a lecture or sequence of lectures;
- to do some shared research into a particular issue or set of issues and so on.

The possibilities are many, and be creative in your thinking and your use of time. Above all, though, remember how important it is that you and your partner are clear of the outcomes you expect of your work together, as this will be the means by which you measure the success of your joint studies.

By working closely with a study partner over extended periods of time, you will find synergies that would be unavailable to you working alone. Needless to say, the amount of reading that can be undertaken by two is greater than the amount that can be undertaken by one. Key texts can be recommended or summarised in note form for each other in order to maximise your time. The experience of summarising and feeding back to your partner will improve your abilities as a reader and will also help develop your skills as a speaker within a mutually supportive and non-threatening environment. This will in turn build your confidence to contribute to discussion in lectures and seminars.

Aside from the purely academic advantages suggested above, working closely with a partner, or a group of partners covering different modules, will provide you with a valuable support structure for when the going gets tough. The development of close working and personal relationships will provide you with an important alternative channel for sorting out difficulties, aside from the formal departmental channels.

STUDYING IN LARGER GROUPS

Many of the advantages of paired study also apply to group study. The larger group format, however, brings advantages and disadvantages of its own. The primary advantage is that a larger group provides a larger pool of ideas and perspectives on whatever is under consideration. There are also disadvantages to working in larger groups, however:

- the logistics of finding a time which is mutually convenient for all group members are more complicated;
- finding a space that is suitable for meeting can be difficult – depending on the size of group you anticipate and the formality, a room in halls, a coffee bar or pub, or a library study room may be appropriate;
- depending on the nature of the group and the material to be covered, the difficulty of location may be overcome by using e-learning environments and chat room facilities at pre-arranged times;

- agreeing on a shared focus for the group – this is obviously more difficult than in a pair, as more needs and interests have to be met;
- sharing out the leadership of sessions, so that the burden does not fall too heavily on a few individuals;
- deciding corporately upon the outcomes for group sessions and how they will be distributed to all group members.

Meetings of the group may be formal or informal. Sometimes just meeting together informally to chat about reading – related or unrelated to the modules you are studying – may be important. This will keep your passion and enthusiasm for your subject alive, even if you are studying some modules that seem heavy going. Reading for study and reading for pleasure are not necessarily synonymous, and if you are to succeed and be happy in your studies, it is essential that reading remains a pleasurable activity for you. Discussing issues and texts not directly covered by what you are studying can sometimes raise illuminating issues and comparisons, and also helps you to develop your breadth of understanding and knowledge as a student of literature.

Where there is a more formal agenda, it is important to agree upon a weekly schedule for contribution. This maintains a sense of purpose and structure in your group meetings. On a weekly basis, individuals or small groups should take responsibility for leading discussion. This will ensure that the responsibility of running these sessions does not fall too heavily upon any one person and will enable you to gain input and ideas from more group members.

Student input into seminars (and even occasionally lectures) is a common feature of university work and can be quite intimidating. Discussion in seminars can be energetic and exciting, especially when many members of the group come well prepared and ready to air their ideas. Where students are under prepared, though (let us say they have not done the required reading), or when they are nervous and unwilling to contribute, it can also be a rather unsatisfying experience. By contributing regularly within a peer study group, you can develop your confidence and skills as a speaker. You can also use group sessions to develop ideas you may wish to contribute to lectures and seminars. Taking responsibility for leading group study sessions will also give you an insight into the experience of your lecturers and seminar leaders, the choices and difficulties they face in preparing teaching sessions. This will help you understand the processes of teaching and learning more clearly.

USING THE LIBRARY

The university library is a place with which you will rapidly become familiar. As a student of English Literature you will have extensive reading lists and will have to cover a wide range of reading from early on in your course. Guidance on how to interpret and work with reading lists can be found in Chapter 6. There will be certain texts and resources that you will be advised to purchase because you will use them repeatedly throughout your course. Others you will need or want to purchase for yourself, as you may wish to annotate them or retain them for your own personal use. However, for many reference works, books of literary theory, journals and other secondary sources you will rely on the university library. It is worth remembering that every other student on your course is in the same boat. Many university English Literature courses attract large numbers of students. There will also be students following combined honours programmes who will need access to the same bank of materials, and general readers who may wish to borrow some of the books you may wish to use. Although more and more texts, both primary and secondary, are available online (see pp. 176–7 and pp. 185–6), the demand placed on library resources is therefore likely to be very heavy, and no institution can possibly hold stocks of texts for all students.

For this reason, it is essential that you leave yourself plenty of time in advance of deadlines to locate, borrow and use library resources. Pressure on materials, especially key recommended texts and journals, obviously becomes very heavy in the immediate run-up to submission deadlines. If you are not careful you can run into difficulties, needing to borrow resources which are simply not available (or available for only very limited times) owing to demand. For this reason it is important to make sure that you structure your library time and develop a long-term view of what you need to use. Module handbooks will include recommended reading lists and other key resources, and you should make sure that you approach these systematically throughout the module to avoid falling into the 'last minute' trap. Another reason to make sure you plan your library use ahead is that many popular and high-demand items will be on restricted loan (normally only of a few hours) to ensure that access to them is fairly shared around. The likelihood of these items being available is clearly greater early in the module cycle than it will be at a later stage when assignment panic sets in.

Many universities and departments will arrange, as part of your formal induction, a tour of the library. This may, however, be left for you to arrange for yourself. This is a very important part of your introduction to university, as a member of the library staff will show you the relevant sections of the library, how to access electronic resources such as e-journals, and how to make catalogue searches. The sooner these things are mastered, the easier your transition into effective use of the library will be.

VIRTUAL LEARNING ENVIRONMENTS (VLES) AND WEB BASES

VLEs and a wide range of web-based materials are also now available to students of English Literature. Particular advice and protocols surrounding the use of these can be found in Chapter 8.

CONCLUSIONS

Studying independently is more profitable and more stimulating where you make the experience rich and varied. Certainly you must spend time working alone – at the end of the day, after all, your English degree tests your abilities as an individual reader and critic – but long hours spent alone are isolating, and can lead to uncertainty and misconceptions. If you supplement your individual study by meeting regularly in pairs or groups, the work you do on your own is enriched. The study of English requires dialogue and debate. Creating a well-balanced and varied pattern of independent study should lead to an increase both in your knowledge of your subject and in your confidence as a participant in teaching sessions.

4 Seminars and workshops

By the end of this chapter you will have considered:

- the purpose of seminars and workshops in your degree;
- how seminars relate to lectures;
- your roles and responsibilities in seminars and workshops;
- how to prepare for seminars and workshops;
- how to use module handbooks;
- giving presentations in seminars and workshops.

INTRODUCTION

In the course of your English Literature degree, it is likely that you will spend many hours in seminars. Perhaps less common, but still an important part of English Literature degrees, are workshops. This chapter aims to offer you insight into both seminars and workshops and to explore what you can expect from them. It will look at how each relates to lectures and to your independent study, suggesting some of the ways you can effectively prepare for them.

Seminars and workshops can be very varied in both their form and content. They are normally, though not always, linked to a lecture, and provide you with the opportunity to explore through discussion and a range of other activities what you have learned from the lecture and your independent study. The connection between a lecture and a seminar may be direct – a seminar on Shakespeare's tragedy *Titus Andronicus* following on from a lecture on that play, for example. A seminar may also explore, through a discussion of specific texts, generic issues – a seminar on *The Great Gatsby*, for instance, may follow a lecture on the American Dream. Alternatively, a seminar may address other texts related to a text covered in a lecture – a discussion of *Valperga* and *The Last Man*, two lesser known novels by Mary Shelley, after a lecture on *Frankenstein*, for example. The connection between lecture and seminar may be related to period – a seminar on Wilkie Collins' novels *The Woman in White* and *Armadale*, for instance, may well follow on from a lecture on the Victorian novel. Genre may provide another focus – the same two Collins novels may be discussed as examples of Victorian sensation fiction. Likewise, a workshop on an episode of *The Singing Detective* may explore further issues raised in a lecture on television drama. Seminars and workshops may, however, be free-standing, or may relate to lectures in tangential ways. The possibilities are almost endless.

What all seminars and workshops should have in common, however, is that they provide an opportunity for you to explore in a more interactive way issues relating to your study of literature. Lectures are not, by their very nature, suited to open discussion. Hopefully your lecturers will find some way to engage you and your peers in something more than listening, but this will still be limited. Even if lecturers offer the chance for brief discussion, or take questions during lectures, the opportunity for you to engage in detailed discussion of what they are saying is limited. In seminars and workshops you have your chance to speak out.

SEMINARS AND WORKSHOPS – WHAT'S THE DIFFERENCE?

Seminars and workshops are both small group teaching formats. Small, that is, compared to lectures, which are often delivered to very large cohorts of students, especially in the first year when many universities run core programmes that all students follow. Even though seminars and workshops are considered small teaching groups, you may well find that these groups are still bigger than many of your A level, IB or Access classes. Seminar and workshop groups often consist of up to 30 students. So, while in one sense this will be the most familiar kind of teaching you will encounter, it is still quite different in a number of ways to what you will have encountered before.

Before we go on to explore briefly how workshops and seminars differ from one another, it is worthwhile identifying a few key factors that relate generally to this aspect of your teaching and learning at university:

- the seminar or workshop group is likely to be much larger than your classes at A level, Access or IB;
- you will probably be part of a number of different seminar or workshop groups (e.g. for Shakespeare, the novel, poetry, Middle English), whereas at school or college you probably remained in the same teaching group for all aspects of your course;
- because of both of the above points, the social dynamics of groups and your role within them will change from one seminar or workshop to another;
- the pace at which material is covered will be significantly faster – typically, a seminar or workshop will cover one text (sometimes even more) per week;
- your ability to participate in seminars or workshops will depend to a considerable extent upon the effectiveness of your preparatory independent study;
- seminar leaders may well set preparatory tasks in the way of reading or other activity that they will expect you to complete before coming to a seminar – these should always be completed, otherwise you will not be able to participate effectively;
- you will usually have been given much preparatory material for a seminar or workshop before it begins by means of a plenary lecture – you will be expected to make use of these ideas, developing and applying them within the course of the seminar or workshop.

The nature of workshops and seminars can, as we discovered at the beginning of this chapter, be very varied in structure and purpose. However, some useful generalisations can be made, and it is important to be clear about some key distinctions between seminars and workshops. These are summarised in Figure 4.1

Seminars	Workshops
Often *discussion based* around a central text or issue, sometimes including a range of other activities	Often *practically based*, involving discussion, creative work and a range of other activities
Require substantial pre-reading, often of primary texts (e.g. *The House of Dr Dee*, Peter Ackroyd) and secondary texts (e.g. *The Survey of London*, John Stow)	Will require pre-reading of a variety of types (e.g. primary texts, secondary texts, and other students' work)
Independent study prior to session will often be specified, possibly including a range of preparatory activities	Independent study will often require individual or group writing and circulation of this prior to the workshop
Seminar will require follow-up note-making, exploratory writing, further reading, etc.	Workshop will require follow-up recording, further reading, redrafting of practical work, etc.

Figure 4.1 Seminars and workshops

Seminars, then, tend to be discussion based. Workshops will also involve discussion, but will also involve creative work. Whether discussion- or creatively-based, though, both require active engagement from students if they are to work effectively and to provide fulfilling and useful learning experiences. This may seem rather an obvious observation, but in both seminars and workshops it is possible to 'hide'. As indicated above, the size of seminar and workshop groups is often large compared to A level, Access or IB classes, and group leaders may not press you to contribute. You are, after all, adults, and will be expected to motivate yourself to become involved. All too often, though, you find seminar and workshop rooms where it seems only a comparatively small number of students arrived prepared to join in. Lack of participation is very frustrating for lecturers and also for other members of the group, who are there wishing to develop fruitful and academically challenging debate about the subject of study.

Here is what one first-year student has to say about her experience of seminars:

> At first – even now – in a seminar group of 15 people, six people talk and everyone else sits by themselves and doesn't say anything. And it's just a shame, because the six people that are talking are airing their views and then the people that are quiet are taking everything down, but the people that don't talk, they're not giving off what they think, so it's not a two-way thing, and that's not fair on the people who are talking, because they're not getting anything back, so the argument doesn't get explored as much as it could be.

Her frustration is evident and understandable.

Non-participation does nothing to help you progress and develop your understanding. If you do not participate in discussion and activity in a seminar or workshop, it is unlikely that your personal questions and interests will be addressed, and this will limit your learning. Obviously this does not make sense. It is worth making the effort to overcome native shyness and nervousness so that you can gain the maximum. Often non-participation arises from a lack of preparation for seminars and workshops. This can arise from laziness, but is often because students find it difficult to organise their reading and study time efficiently. Chapter 3 provides a lot of helpful guidance for getting yourself organised. You owe it to your seminar or workshop leaders, your peers and yourself to make sure that you are well prepared and that you take an active role in the process of the teaching session. Otherwise it can become an unsatisfactory experience for all concerned.

LECTURE INTO SEMINAR/WORKSHOP

The principle behind much university teaching is for an introductory lecture followed by a related seminar or workshop. The lecture will be used to set out some of the major ideas in relation to a particular text, the work of a particular author, a genre or a literary period. These ideas are then followed up in seminars or workshops.

Themes may be developed across sequences of lectures and seminars. In a course on the Romantic poets, for example, not all aspects of Romanticism will be covered in the first lecture, but will be spread across a number of lectures and applied to the work of a range of poets (e.g. Wordsworth, Coleridge, Shelley and Byron). As discussed in Chapter 5, your role as a student here is to reflect both backwards and forwards through the sequence of lectures, using your independent study to apply ideas raised in the lectures more generally across the poetry you have studied. Ideas raised in a lecture in Week 4, for example, may need to be applied to works discussed in the lecture in Weeks 1, 2 and 3 as well.

> The lecture and seminar style works very well, I feel, as the lecture throws lots of ideas out and the seminar is a chance to develop or ask questions about them.

Seminars and workshops have a central role to play as you develop your understanding. But first a brief word of explanation. These will not necessarily be led by the person who gives the weekly lecture, but may well be led by other members of staff and PhD students, who are often given teaching responsibilities in university. These lecturers will be charged with developing your understanding in relation to the module you are studying. Sometimes seminar and workshop leaders will be working according to a set programme of texts and issues common to all seminar groups, but this is not always the case. Sometimes seminar leaders will choose passages for study, texts, authors and other materials according to their own preferences, expertise and research interests. Provided that the materials covered enable you to deepen your understanding of the area of literature you are studying this is not a problem. It is part of the variety you should expect and value at university.

Seminars and workshops provide an opportunity for you to explore issues arising either from your independent studies or from a preparatory lecture. You may have questions that you want to ask, ideas that you want to try out, or connections that you wish to clarify between texts, authors or concepts that you have been studying. In a seminar or workshop you do not have to stay silent – this is your time to talk, so make the most of it. Of course, seminar and workshop leaders have responsibility for running their sessions, and they will have planned agendas for the seminar, but they also have a responsibility to be responsive to your needs. Be thoughtful, though. If you have small questions and ideas you want to explore, these can probably be brought up within the natural flow of discussion in the seminar. If, however, you have major issues that you would like to have clarified or if there is a particular topic you would like to discuss which will take some time to deal with properly, it is probably best (and most courteous) to speak to the seminar or workshop leader outside of the teaching session to see how this can be addressed. You may well be raising important issues that need to be incorporated into later seminars or workshops.

PRESENTATIONS

As part of your input into seminars and workshops you may well be asked to give presentations. These may be on topics of your own choice relating to the module you are studying, but are more likely to be set by the seminar or workshop leader. Such presentations may be made individually, in pairs or in small groups, and are an important part of your learning experience and in your development as a student, as they require you to verbalise in a very public way your understanding of particular topics. In some cases, presentations of this kind may form part of the formal assessment of a module, in which case the stakes may be high.

Making presentations does not only test your understanding of the topic you are addressing, it also develops your skills as a speaker, your ability to work within strict time limits and your abilities to use presentational aids, such as PowerPoint or overhead projectors. If you come from an A-level background this may well come as something of a shock, as oral assessment is not part of the picture at A level. For those of you from an IB background, however, this will be more familiar.

Here are some useful things to think about:

- leave plenty of time for preparation, as synthesising a range of materials and issues into a short time slot is not easy and requires care;
- think carefully about your audience (e.g. Who are they? What do they already know about this topic? What do they want to know about it? What do I want them to know?) and tailor your presentation in response to these questions;
- make sure your presentation is not too long (this is not fair on other groups who are also giving presentations) and not too short (this is very embarrassing and shows lack of preparation and awareness – if the seminar or workshop leader asks for 15 minutes, that is what they want, and they will have planned their session accordingly);
- make your presentation relevant and engaging through the use of appropriate materials;
- amusing anecdotes will make your presentation more engaging, but you should make sure they relate to what you are talking about;
- think carefully about examples you want to use from primary and secondary texts and reference your sources – make sure they show what you want them to show, and think about providing paper copies of them so that other members of the group can follow the examples for themselves;
- if you are planning to read from a text, make sure you have the passages for reading clearly marked so that you do not face the embarrassment of not being able to find them;
- if you are going to use audiovisual (AV) materials, make sure that you have videos and cassettes in the right place or that you know the track and chapter numbers for CDs and DVDs;
- ensure that AV facilities are working before you begin, if this is possible, so that you are not left floundering by a failure of technology;
- think about appropriate stimuli you might use to create interest and extension for your audience (e.g. music, DVD, visual images, objects);
- think about using PowerPoint or some other kind of visual stimulus to provide a summary of your talk as you progress, but make sure this is not a verbatim version of what you are saying,

otherwise your audience may rightly wonder why you did not just put the presentation on and let them read it;

- if possible, avoid reading – your audience will much prefer it if you talk to them rather than read at them;
- if you need the security of having something written down, try using flash cards with the key points of your presentation written down, so that you do not forget the general direction of your presentation;
- make time to practise your presentation – this will help you with keeping properly to time, and will also help you make sure you are saying exactly what you want;
- if possible, have a trial run of your presentation in front of a friend (or video yourself) – this will help you pick up on any poor communication (e.g. never making eye contact with your audience), any verbal mannerisms (e.g. repeated 'errs', 'likes', 'OKs'), and any awkward physical embarrassment (e.g. running your hands through your hair, wiping sweaty hands on your trousers).

ACTIVITY 11

Preparing for presentations

Now that you have read through the guidance, it is time to have a go. Giving presentations is a skill that can be developed over time, and even if you are very nervous at the idea of giving a formal talk in front of your peers and seminar leaders – which is understandable – you can, with practice, learn to overcome your nerves. Being well prepared is 9/10ths of the battle.

Take a text you know very well – perhaps this could be one of the set texts you did for A level or IB, or a text you have already studied as part of your degree. Prepare a ten-minute presentation explaining why you find this text particularly appealing, and why you would recommend it for study to a group of your peers, commenting on any aspect of the text (e.g. use of language, central themes, theoretical issues, formal/structural matters, context). You may want to make a PowerPoint presentation.

Deliver the presentation to some of your peers, or if you are too shy to do this, try videoing it, or doing it in front of a mirror.

GROUP DISCUSSIONS

Group discussion is a very worthwhile activity. Figure 4.2 shows how useful most students and lecturers consider it to be. And it is no wonder. For what else did you choose to do an English Literature degree, after all, if not to talk about literature? This can happen, of course, in informal discussions with your peers, but seminars and workshops also provide an excellent forum for this meeting of minds. They are learning spaces where discussion can take place, guided by your lecturers. In this context, a wide range of views can be aired, and the seminar or workshop leader can direct thinking about them. This is something that you should find very valuable. Where discussion is engaging, seminars and workshops will lead you into a wider and more connected understanding of the texts you are studying and of literature in general. They will enable you to widen your personal responses, to expand your knowledge and to apply practically a range of theoretical and contextual issues surrounding them. In addition, seminars and workshops provide a perfect opportunity to exchange, develop and test out ideas. These may come from your independent study or from a preparatory lecture.

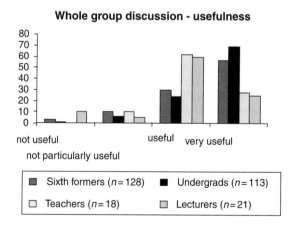

Figure 4.2 How useful is whole group discussion?

Source: Green, A. (2005). *Four Perspectives on Transition: English Literature from Sixth Form to University.* Higher Education Academy English Subject Centre: Royal Holloway, University of London.

However, difficulties can also arise. If discussion in the whole group context is ill-guided, it can become irrelevant or confusing. There can also be the tendency for some students to dominate discussion. These problems are most likely to arise when students are either unwilling or unable (probably because of poor preparation) to contribute to the debate.

The most important thing to remember about seminars and workshops is that, unlike lectures, which are by and large solo efforts, they depend upon co-operation and contribution from all present if they are to be successful learning environments. But in reality, it is very easy to remain anonymous in seminars. Non-participation is a clear (if not desirable) option. When students choose not to participate, the purpose of the seminar or workshop is rather defeated. Students find lack of participation by their peers frustrating, as seminars and workshops rely on the participation of all members of the group.

> I could go into a seminar, say, and I could sit there silent for the whole thing and not be questioned. I don't think that's really helpful. I think it's nice to be able to get all of this information and ideas out from the group and then be able to collectively use them.

BE PREPARED

Perhaps one of the most important reasons why students do not participate in seminars and workshops as effectively as they might is lack of suitable preparation. It may seem on the surface that seminars are an informal chat, but unless you have prepared effectively, it is a chat you will find it difficult to be involved in. Preparation is very important for seminars and workshops. Make sure that you have done any pre-reading tasks and other activities your lecturer has set – they will form an important part of the discussion and you will be disadvantaged if you have not done so. Use your handbook to help you think in advance about the issues the seminar is going to cover. Make some initial notes and take them with you to the seminar. Maybe even devise a sheet for taking notes in the session.

If you are attending a seminar following up on a lecture keep a note of any questions that you were not able to ask the lecturer. You may have an opportunity to raise them in your seminar, either formally in a question and answer slot or by bringing the questions into group discussion.

Here is an extract from the handbook for a first-year module on Shakespeare's History plays. It provides discussion focuses and suggested reading for weekly seminars on *Henry IV Part 1* and *Henry V*:

I Henry IV

Topics and Issues for Discussion
Is this play critical and subversive of political authority, or is it actually very conservative? Why is the relationship between Prince Hal and his father so strained? What's Hal playing at? What is Falstaff's role in the play, and what's Hotspur's?

Further reading
C. L. Barber, *Shakespeare's Festive Comedy* (New Jersey: Princeton University Press, 1959), ch. 8.

Phyllis Rackin, *Stages of History: Shakespeare's English Chronicles* (Ithaca: Cornell University Press, 1990).

Kiernan Ryan, 'The future of history: 1 and 2 *Henry IV*', in *Shakespeare* (Hemel Hempstead: Prentice Hall, 1991).

Derek Cohen, '*Henry IV Part 1*: rituals of violence', in *Shakespeare's History Plays*, ed. Graham Holderness (London: Macmillan, 1992).

Nigel Wood (ed.), *Theory in Practice: Henry IV* (Buckingham: Open University Press, 1995).

Henry V

Topics and Issues for Discussion
How has the character of Henry developed in *Henry IV Part 1* and *Henry V*? What does it mean to be 'English' in the play? Is the play supportive or critical of warfare? How are we to interpret Henry's marriage to Katherine? What do we make of the play's patriotic beliefs today? What is the role of Pistol? Why is there so little 'real action' in the play?

➢

Further reading

Ewan Fernie, 'Action! *Henry V*', in *Presentist Shakespeare*, ed. Hugh Grady and Terence Hawkes (London and New York: Routledge, 2006).

Annabel Patterson, *Shakespeare and the Popular Voice* (Oxford: Blackwell, 1989), ch. 4.

Willy Maley, '"This sceptred isle": Shakespeare and the British problem', in *Shakespeare and National Culture*, ed. John Joughin, Manchester University Press (Manchester, 1997).

Jonathan Dollimore and Alan Sinfield, 'History and ideology: *Henry V*', in *Shakespeare's History Plays*, ed. Graham Holderness (London: Macmillan, 1992).

Graham Holderness, '"What ish my nation?": Shakespeare and national identities', *Textual Practice* 5 (1991), 74–93.

Graham Holderness, 'Agincourt 1944: readings in the Shakespeare myth', *Literature and History*, 10 (1984), 24–45.

ACTIVITY 12

Preparing for a seminar

Look carefully at the handbook extracts above. How would you set about preparing for these seminars? What other sources of information may you need to consult? What questions would you want answered as you went into the seminar? You may find it helpful to use the KWL grid explained in Appendix 1.

If you have undertaken this sort of thoughtful preparation for seminars and workshops, you should feel confident to participate in discussion and any other activities. You will also have taken control of your own learning, proactively thinking about how your needs and questions can be addressed. Through this you will effectively engage with texts and concepts in a more meaningful way. This is particularly important in a subject like English Literature, where teaching hours are short.

WORKSHOPS

Workshops are distinctly different from seminars. Whilst they are still often discussion based, the whole idea behind workshops, as their name suggests, is about creation and creativity. This is not to say that creative thought and creative activity do not have their place in seminars and even in lectures, but the primary purpose of workshops is to lead to creative outcomes. For this reason they are often employed in creative writing courses, which you may well have the opportunity to follow as part of your degree.

Here is an example outline from a creative writing module on novel writing. In order to ensure that all students gain the same basic input, note that the week begins with a plenary lecture, where the main issues for the week are outlined, and where any major theoretical concepts are introduced to everybody. The remainder of the work, however, is undertaken in smaller workshop groups. The passage below identifies some of the processes involved in small group work, and explains the relationship between this and the more formal lecture which begins the week:

Each week there will be a plenary lecture given to all the students taking this module, after which you will move into small groups for workshops and presentations. In the first half of the semester we begin to define good writing and the techniques that create it and to strengthen your mastery of language. You will be set a creative exercise every week and asked to circulate what you write to your workshop group for their feedback.

As the semester progresses, interactive exercises and individual writing will be combined to use your powers of observation, listening and conceptualising in writing prose fiction. Working in small presentation groups, you will compare the way different contemporary writers approach the core elements of fiction writing, discuss these and practice the same techniques yourselves. You will begin to establish and become aware of your own writing processes and at the end of the module you will be able to discuss these in a brief individual presentation.

To demonstrate how workshops may look in practice, here are two weekly session outlines from a module on writing drama:

Week 1
Course overview
Why is theatre important? What role has the theatre played in society?
What is a play and what sets theatre apart from other performing arts?
What are the unique advantages of the form?
The monologue – writing for one voice.

Assignment: write a 600-word monologue
You will have one week to write each assignment and these will be workshopped the week after they are set. Your first workshop session will be devoted to a screening and discussion.

Week 2
Getting Started. How plays are structured and formatted. Theatrical conventions and craft. The creative team: writing for your directors, designers and actors.

Assignment: write stage directions and an opening scene.

The first week, you will notice, is given over to establishing the ground to be covered in the course. But in the following weeks the nature of teaching and what students are expected to do change. Teaching begins to focus on the mechanics of the theatre and the particular demands of writing for it. Each stage of the teaching process is accompanied by structured creative writing tasks to be workshopped the following week. This requires students within workshop groups to circulate their writing in advance so that the other members of the group have the chance to read and reflect on the work before the workshop session, and have thought through any observations and comments they wish to make.

This type of work places particular demands upon students. First we should note the advantages:

- through the structured process of undertaking the small writing tasks, students are steadily introduced to the component parts of stage plays and screenplays;
- repeated opportunities are provided for the students to explore their ideas on a small canvas, focussing in on specified aspects of the process of drama writing (e.g. monologue, stage directions, dialogue);
- the weekly short writing extracts are discussed in the workshop group and constructive criticisms are made for development;
- these small pieces can, if students choose to make them, build their writing systematically towards their final submitted work.

There are other issues to consider, though:

- reliability is very important – for workshops to work well, every member of the group must always attend;
- the other members of your group will be relying on you to provide constructive feedback on their work – you must make sure all reading and preparation is done in time for the workshop;
- you must make sure that work is always circulated on time to allow other members of the workshop group time to read it – if you do not do so, all members of the group will suffer: you will not have your work commented on, and the trust of the group will be broken;
- you may well feel vulnerable – putting your writing into the public forum of a workshop, where it is available for others to comment on can be hard: writing is personal, and it is some-times hard to have it publicly discussed, but your confidence will grow as time progresses;
- workshop groups rely on trust – criticism of others' work should always be constructive (i.e. given with the intention of helping them to improve, and preferably accompanied by an alternative suggestion);

- destructive criticism can break down other students' confidence and also breaks down the trust within the group – this limits the effectiveness of the workshop group.

ACTIVITY 13

Giving constructive criticism

Read the following passage, which has been written as the opening to a thriller. Imagine it is a piece that has been circulated by one of your group members for discussion at the next workshop.

You have been told to focus your comments on:

pace; atmosphere; vocabulary; uncertainty.

Jot down the constructive criticisms you would make. Select specific examples from the text and think carefully about what you want to say. Select both examples you think are good and examples you think could benefit from improvement – remember to have alternative suggestions for these.

How do you think this process would benefit:

The writer of the passage? Other students in the group? Yourself?

Prologue – Events

I

He held the book in his hand and scanned the room. Light from the late afternoon sun filtered into the chamber through a dirty window high up on one wall. It would soon be dark. He had to be quick and he needed more light. He went to the table that stood in the middle of the room and lit a candle which had been crudely stuffed into the neck of a bottle.

That done, unhurried and calm, he turned his mind to the obvious question. Where should he leave it? He could not just leave it on some random shelf. The success of his plans depended on choosing precisely the right spot. He had to make his choice with the mind of the poet.

He did a quick circuit of the room. There were texts in all of the main European languages. The answer came to him easily enough. It would be best with the other texts in English.

He returned to the shelves where he had seen the English books and quickly read over the titles. Again the answer supplied itself. There was only one place it could go. Next to Milton.

Yes.

He slipped the book on to the shelf.

*

'Morose,' said The Poet, 'never seen him in any other state.'

The Dean, accompanying the great man nodded in a non-committal sort of way and sucked again at the rim of his crystal sherry glass. He flicked a glance across from under his peppery eyebrows to the person under discussion. Professor Marshall – rounded shoulders, gown sprinkled with dandruff, crumpled trousers. His dour eyes and hangdog expression, the thinning, once-ginger hair now grey, and his pallid-as-parchment face all certainly, the Dean had to admit, contributed to The Poet's observation that he was, indeed, morose. The Dean, however, did not necessarily subscribe to all The Poet's particular perspectives.

'Who's he with?' The Poet peered across the Hall, which was now concertedly rumbling with a hundred Donnish conversations.

The Dean peered with him, glad to escape the need to actually agree with The Poet. 'Looks like Freeman,' he said, correctly identifying the younger man in glasses who was dressed, beneath his gown, in a rusty corduroy suit and desert boots – his unruly, nut brown hair sprayed in all directions, making him look as if he'd only just got up.

Professor Marshall became aware that he was being watched. As his eyes latched onto The Poet's, his gloomy countenance was replaced by something not far from active dislike, if not venom. Although Professor Marshall, despite his demeanour, was probably not capable of actual venom. His was not an unkind soul. However, there was something about The Poet that rankled, and brought out the worst in him.

In fact, Professor Marshall, only a few minutes earlier, as they had wandered into Hall for the pre-dinner reception, had slid alongside The Poet and made clear his views.

'You have been weighed, tested and found wanting,' the academic had muttered to The Poet under his breath.

➤

The Poet sneered in response, not deigning to turn and look at his accuser. He had initially taken the remark as a manifestation of jealousy. He was about to be honoured by his illustrious peers at this rather splendid dinner; glittering with silver and chandeliers. An honour he had, it was true to say, felt he utterly deserved. It was doubtful Professor Marshall would ever be so honoured.

No wonder.

Miserable old fool.

Yet, on further reflection, The Poet had begun to question his initial reaction. Had the academic's bitter remark anything to do with previous conversations they'd had last year, during Trinity term?

And why was he now standing talking to Freeman?

It looked like conspiracy to The Poet. How much did Marshall know? How much was he telling Freeman?

Freeman of all people?

*

There was a loud beep, a number flashed. Up ahead the woman at the front of the queue moved to a vacant cashier. Slowly everybody who was waiting inched forwards to fill up the space she had left.

Three places back in the line stood Professor Marshall. Under his arm he held two packages, both wrapped in thick brown paper, neatly tied in a quaintly old-fashioned way with string. There was another beep and the people in front of him shuffled forward to the accompaniment of piped music. It was all curiously impersonal, but in a way he liked that. It was the anonymity of the modern world, and anonymity had its advantages. He scanned the room with its functional furnishing and its uniform decor – just like almost every other post office up and down the country.

He looked too at the people around him. No-one he knew. That was good. Not that anyone would guess what he was doing from the plain brown package he was about to mail, mind you. What could be so unusual about a man in his sixties, wearing a beige raincoat with a greasy collar, posting a package? But nevertheless he was somehow pleased to be alone. Soon he would be at the desk and the precious package would be on its way.

He took the parcels from under his arm to read the addresses carefully once more, methodical and precise as ever. The addresses were printed on labels. Something had told him that it was best to avoid the possibility of his writing being recognised. He cast his critical eye over the words:

Dr Daniel Freeman
Stairwell H.
Trinity College
Cambridge

and the second package:

Dr Daniel Freeman
Flat 8
Six Steps
95 Tenison Rd
Cambridge
CB1 2DJ

Yes. It was all accurate. He did not want to take any risks with the contents going astray. Many things hung on its successful delivery.

Suddenly he felt a tap on his shoulder. He had been concentrating so hard on the package that he had missed the movements of the queue ahead of him. He quickly thanked the man who had been standing behind him and who, unknown to him, had clearly read the destination of the package. He faced the counter again. The number 6 was flashing on the screen, accompanied by an insistent beep. It was his turn. As quickly as he could he made his way to the counter. The girl behind the glass stared at him and waited for him to initiate the transaction. *How the world has changed* he thought fleetingly before he spoke. 'Recorded Delivery, please.'

SEMINARS AND WORKSHOPS WITHIN THE STUDY CYCLE

It is worth reminding yourself at this stage of the study cycle discussed in Chapter 1.

THE STUDY CYCLE

Now think about how this fits into another cycle of study:

The Study cycle

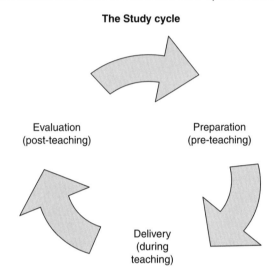

Evaluation
(post-teaching)

Preparation
(pre-teaching)

Delivery
(during
teaching)

As you begin to think about how the different component parts of your study of English Literature fit together, you can identify at what points cycles of study start to overlap. You need, for example, to do preparatory work before you attend a lecture – this is more fully discussed in Chapter 5, and then to reflect on the material presented in that lecture. These processes in themselves, however, also become part of the process of preparing for a seminar or workshop. Likewise, reflection on the outcomes of a seminar become preparation for a forthcoming lecture. The sooner you are able to understand the ways in which the various elements of your study come together, the sooner you will understand the holistic nature of university study, and the ways in which you can begin to make connections between the different aspects of your studies.

CONCLUSIONS

Seminars and workshops are a very important part of the experience of studying for your English Literature degree. They are an ideal opportunity for you to explore ideas emerging from both lectures and your independent studies. Unlike in most lectures, in seminars and workshops you will have ample opportunity – if you choose to use it – to discuss your own ideas and to use this as a springboard for deepening and broadening your understanding. It is essential to spend time properly preparing for seminars and workshops and to undertake all preparatory readings and tasks, as otherwise you will not be able to participate fully, and this is a significant waste of opportunity. Remember, seminars work best when everyone is prepared to participate.

5 Lectures

By the end of this chapter you will have considered:

- how to prepare for lectures using module handbooks;
- how to pre-plan note-taking;
- how to work in lectures;
- how to follow up on lectures;
- how to deal with questions;
- transition from lecture to seminar and workshops;
- how to develop lecture notes – note-taking into note-making.

INTRODUCTION

The majority of students view lectures as a key source of learning. Perhaps this is because of an understandable lack of confidence in their own ability to construct knowledge. After all, faced with the words of an expert, most young students naturally tend to hold on to lectures as a very important part of their learning. The often large and faceless nature of lectures also offers security and the opportunity to take copious notes. This may also be related to the low number of contact hours typical of English degree courses, which encourages students to cling tightly to the valued contact time they have and to see the input of the lecturer at the heart of this. Perhaps you can relate to this.

But lectures are also problematic. How do they relate to and help you in your independent study? How do you select and evaluate information given in lectures? How do you relate the information you gather in one lecture to your learning in other areas of your course? What do you do if you have a question? The purpose of this chapter is to address these questions and more so that you can think more effectively about how best to operate as a learner in the lecture theatre.

PREPARING FOR LECTURES

It is important to think carefully about what you can do to prepare yourself for lectures. Too often students turn up at lectures without having done anything meaningful (if anything at all) in the way of preparation. The impersonal nature of lectures, which are often given to large numbers of students, can encourage this. Whilst failure to prepare effectively undoubtedly does not help with your understanding, it is unlikely that lack of preparation will be exposed in the way it might in a seminar.

> I guess there is a tendency for lectures not to worry too much, because you know you're never going to get picked on or asked to do something or speak about something. And quite often by the time you've had your lecture, you can go to the seminar and you feel much better about it anyway because you've learnt in the lecture that you've just had. But I don't know if preparing for lectures any more than the notes in the handbook... I don't know.

Lack of effective preparation is not always down to lack of dedication and interest, though. Often it results from lack of understanding of how best to do so.

> When I've spent time preparing it has given me more confidence to question what's being said and I feel more engaged with what's happening whereas the times that I haven't done it it's felt like I'm just sitting here taking notes and the thing gets passive rather than active.

PREPARING FOR LECTURES USING MODULE HANDBOOKS

> To be honest, I don't think I really prepare. I just try and read the text before or get through as much of it as I can. Because I don't know what to prepare. I just go in a take notes and put them in my folder really.

Let us consider an example of how you might set about preparing for lectures. It uses a first-year module on Shakespeare as an example. As we have already seen in Chapter 3, module handbooks provide you with a wealth of useful information. Let us look again at the introductory section of the module handbook:

> This course will introduce you to the close study of a wide range of Shakespeare's plays. The objective of the course is to facilitate a deeper – as well as a more pleasurable and rewarding – understanding of the range of Shakespeare's work. The course is broadly chronological. In this first semester we will concentrate on the genres of comedy and history, before going on to study the tragedies and romances next semester. As the course progresses, you will be encouraged to think about the plays as theatre as well as printed literature; but a main feature of the course will be its close attention to the extraordinary fertility and force of Shakespeare's dramatic language. While paying some attention to Shakespeare's very different historical context in the Renaissance, we will be equally concerned with the question of whether the plays are still relevant to us today. By the end of the course, you should have developed a good working knowledge of Shakespeare's dramatic and literary craft and be able to think and write intelligently, confidently and creatively about the plays.

This informs you that the purpose of the module is to introduce you to the close study of a wide range of Shakespeare's plays and 'to facilitate a deeper understanding' of the plays. By implication the purpose of lectures and seminars is introductory. They are not intended to be the extent of your engagement with the plays.

Lectures are intended to introduce you to the kind of close readings that you should develop through your personal studies.

> The lecture is a way of introducing you to key concepts and ideas in relation to each of the texts studied; but it is a first rather than the last word on Shakespeare. You will have a chance to discuss and debate both the lecture and other relevant issues in your one-hour fortnightly seminar following the lecture.

When you are in lectures you should not simply take down every word the lecturer says, but prepare yourself for further study by jotting down questions, references and ideas to think about later. This is an exciting process as it allows you to take much more control of your own learning than you have probably been allowed to date. It is also something that, if you are to do it effectively, you must have thought about before the lecture even begins. It is no good turning up at a lecture ready simply to react to whatever the lecturer may say. What you get out of a lecture is often proportional to the work you put in beforehand. If you go in having already read around the subject – and not only the text that the lecture happens to be about – and with ideas related to the major issues the lecturer will be dealing with, then you will find the experience of the lecture much more stimulating and your learning much more efficient. Module handbooks can really help you here.

The module handbook for the Shakespeare module we are discussing provides a week-by-week outline. Here the broad aims and objectives presented in the introduction are fleshed out to give you a more detailed guide for preparation and study. Here is the outline for a lecture on *The Merchant of Venice*:

> **Week One** *Introduction: The Merchant of Venice I*
>
> *Topics and Issues for Discussion*
> Why does Shakespeare matter? How the course will run. How to get most out of it. *The Merchant of Venice*. Is the play a comedy? How important are the issues of trade and finance to the play? What does
>
> ➤

the play value? What is its view of 'aliens' and 'outsiders'? What is
its view of love or of revenge?

Further reading

Martin Coyle, ed. *The Merchant of Venice* (London: Macmillan,
1998).

James Shapiro, *Shakespeare and the Jews* (New York: Columbia
University Press, 1996).

Thomas Moisan, ' "Which is the merchant here? And which the
Jew?" ': subversion and recuperation in *The Merchant of Venice*,
in *Shakespeare Reproduced: The Text in History and Ideology*,
ed. Jean Howard and Marion O'Connor (London and New York:
Routledge, 1987).

Walter Cohen, '*The Merchant of Venice* and the possibilities of historical criticism', in *Materialist Shakespeare: A History*, ed. Ivo
Kamps (London and New York: Verso, 1995).

Kiernan Ryan, *Shakespeare* (Hemel Hempstead: Prentice Hall,
1991), 17–27.

This outline gives you a set of key issues the lecture will cover and
serves a number of purposes. It could be used as a set of note-
taking headings. Figure 5.1 illustrates how these could be turned
into a simple note-taking sheet. Such note-taking sheets have the
advantage that they keep all your thoughts on a particular aspect
of the play together. This makes working with your notes after
the lecture easier, as you convert your jottings into a fuller set
of notes.

The information in the module handbook could also guide your
reading and thinking prior to the lecture. Some of the points identified are of a broad nature: 'Why does Shakespeare matter?', for
example, asks us to think about Shakespeare as a cultural phe-
nomenon, the value we place upon his writings and why. You will
need to reflect on personal, cultural and literary values. Others lend
themselves to some initial exploratory reading. 'Is the play a comedy', for instance, requires some initial research into what comedy
means in the context of the theatre and in relation to Shakespeare
in particular. Still others guide you to specific issues in the play.

Why does Shakespeare matter?	
Is *The Merchant of Venice* a comedy?	
Trade and Finance	
What does the play value?	
'Aliens' and 'outsiders'	
Love	
Revenge	

Figure 5.1 Note-taking sheet

The final four questions all do this. As you can see, the module handbook provides you with a lot of guidance in preparing for lectures and shows you how personal study time can be used. This is supplemented by a targeted reading list of a handful of texts which focus specifically on the play and the issues to be covered.

Another session outline guides you in a very different way. It does not provide detailed questions for consideration, but instead relates the lecture to two of the broad rationales of the module.

Week Two   *The Merchant of Venice 2*

This special lecture will introduce performance approaches to Shakespeare, focussing on post-Holocaust interpretations of *The Merchant*.

By highlighting 'performance approaches' and 'post-Holocaust interpretations' it draws your attention to the play as theatre, and to cultural-historical issues both at the time of the play's composition and today. This lecture obviously requires a totally different kind of preparation.

ACTIVITY 14

Shakespeare lecture

- What do you think is meant by 'performance approaches'?
- What other academic disciplines does this session seem to cross over with?
- What could you do, either individually or in a group, to prepare for this session?

Through this worked example you can see how module handbooks can prepare you for your studies in a structured and meaningful way. The more carefully you use these suggestions, the more you will get out of independent study in preparation for lectures and from the lectures themselves.

I found it quite daunting because you're just being spoken to the whole time and if you've got a question you either write it down and then bring it up in the seminar or you leave it which is not always that promising.

To summarise, you should use your study time before teaching sessions to:

- think out your initial responses and to formulate some initial ideas;
- jot down some initial thoughts;
- record key passages from your primary and secondary reading – this will prepare you to take an active part in teaching sessions, and you will be ready to make useful contributions;
- think carefully about how you are going to structure your note-taking – how can you most effectively balance participation with recording discussion for future reference?
- devise some formats for note-taking, perhaps even partially completing these before you go to a lecture, using the module handbook as a guide.

Think carefully about these ideas and then try working through an example or two on your own.

ACTIVITY 15

Preparation for lectures

Below is the information for a variety of weekly lectures on a range of topics. Use this information to think carefully about how you should prepare for the weekly lecture. Some of the outlines provide more detail than others. Reflect upon what questions you may wish to follow up. Also think about how you could structure note-taking in the lecture, including recording your initial responses to the topic and/or texts covered.

Week Four   Wordsworth's pastoral: *Michael* and the Lucy poems

Read: Wordsworth, *Michael* [Wu, pp. 346–56], 'Strange Fits of Passion' [Wu, p. 326], 'She Dwelt Among the Untrodden Ways' [Wu, p. 327], 'Three Years She Grew in Sun and Shower' [Wu, p. 328], 'A Slumber Did My Spirit Seal' [Wu, p. 327], 'I Travelled Among Unknown Men' [Wu, p. 356], 'Upon Westminster Bridge' [Wu, p. 374], 'Daffodils' [Wu, p. 383]; Dorothy Wordsworth, excerpts from *Grasmere Journals*, 3 September 1800, 3 October 1800, 15 April 1802, 29 April 1802, and 4 October 1802 [Wu, pp. 433–35]
Lecture: Versions of pastoral; Nature; Urban and countryside vision; Relationship with Dorothy; Lucy and the Grasmere Journals.

Week Three   Fairy Tale I

Fairy tale as oral narrative; fairy tale as literary narrative – literary history of the fairy tale; theories of the fairy tale.

> ## Week Eight   Modernist Theatre
>
> Twentieth-Century Theatre: The Flight from Naturalism, I (expressionist and verse drama; theatre of cruelty; epic theatre: Brecht, *Mother Courage and Her Children*). Marxist approaches and the theatre. Non-verbal communication: sets, props, costume, lighting. Seminar: Brecht, *Mother Courage*.

> ## Weeks One and Two   *Hamlet*
>
> *Topics and Issues for Discussion:* How does the play dramatise death? What's its view of action? Is it a revenge tragedy? How does it dramatise memory and forgetting? What of the relations between fathers and sons, and between Hamlet and his mother? What's the function of the play within the play?

USING LECTURES

We all learn most effectively through interaction. This may be interpersonal interaction or it may be interaction with a text or the ideas in it. Lectures often do not provide the opportunity for this kind of interaction – although many lecturers will try to include some kind of interactive elements in their teaching. Your preparation is one way in which you can do this, as discussed above. But it is also important to use lectures as the basis for further personal exploration.

CASE STUDY OF A LECTURE

The unfamiliarity of lectures and the limited opportunities for interaction with the material presented means that you may well find it hard at first to manage your individual learning. Here is an example from a first year Shakespeare lecture. This lecture, on *Twelfth Night*, was delivered to the whole first-year cohort and took place early in the academic year. The first half of the lecture was dedicated to an exposition of the key features of Shakespearean comedy. To exemplify what he was saying, the lecturer drew to a large extent on the previous week's lecture on *As You Like It*. The purpose of this was clearly to encourage the students to broaden their conceptualisation of studying Shakespeare.

The lecturer's use of the play within the first half of this lecture was very different from the experiences you have probably had at A level, IB or Access. Instead of treating the play as a set text, he treated the play as one of a number of examples of the true subject of the lecture, which was Shakespearean comedy. This was much more general in its scope, and required the students to engage with broader concepts in reading and approaching the plays. To do this effectively they had to reflect on generic issues of comedy and the features of Shakespearean comedy in particular, rather than focussing specifically on *Twelfth Night* itself. The second half of the lecture moved on to explore the ways in which these generic features are treated within *Twelfth Night*, considering to what extent this reflected the previous week's discussion of *As You Like It* and how it differed from it. The movement of the lecture was from the general (Shakespearean comedy) to the particular (*Twelfth Night*), rather than from the particular to the general, as is often the experience at A level, IB or Access.

It was clear that many students had difficulty in managing this way of framing discussion and managing learning. The early section of the lecture was characterised by a lack of note-taking, as students evidently failed to perceive how the lecturer's discussion related to the play they thought they had come to hear a lecture on and how to locate this in relation to their previous learning. In order to do so, they needed to reconceive the role of generic issues and broad principles in their reading and study of Shakespeare. It was not until the lecturer moved on the second half of the lecture, where he addressed *Twelfth Night* specifically that most students, with an almost audible sigh of relief, took up their pens and began taking notes, having missed the real 'meat' in the lecture.

ACTIVITY 16

Case study

Here are the guidance notes from the module handbook.

Topics and Issues for Discussion: In what ways is the world 'turned upside down' and to what effects? How does the play compare and contrast the households of Olivia and Orsino? Why does Olivia fall in love with Viola/Cesario? Who are the winners and who are the losers? What is Malvolio's role? What does it mean to be 'a woman' in this play? What is Feste's role? In what ways and to what extent is this a happy play?

How might you have dealt with this situation in a lecture? How could you have organised your note-taking? What general issues relating to Shakespearean comedy do the specific questions about *Twelfth Night* raise? What issues would you choose to follow up after this lecture?

USING CRITICAL CONTEXTS

First of all, try to develop critical and theoretical perspectives on what you are studying. These will enable you to 'frame' your learning, and will help you to make sense of your learning within and across modules. There follows a range of critical and theoretical perspectives on Gothic literature. Think carefully about any Gothic texts you may know and jot down your thoughts about how these critical perspectives may relate to them. The first example has been done for you to illustrate the kinds of comment you might make.

GOTHIC LITERATURE

Gothic literature is a form that has proven consistently difficult to define. It has manifested itself in many different places and at many different times. In order to gain a fuller understanding of the form, therefore, it is helpful to bear in mind a range of the critical contexts within which gothic literature has been read.

(1) 'Gothic was the archaic, the pagan, that which was prior to, or resisted the establishment of civilised values and a well-regulated society.' (David Punter, *The Literature of Terror*)

Here, Punter suggests the essential historical connotations of the form; notice the emphasis placed on the importance of the past within Gothic. Typically gothic texts deal with a historical time past (e.g. *The Castle of Otranto* (Horace Walpole), *The Monk* (Matthew Lewis) and *The Mysteries of Udolpho* (Anne Radcliffe). Other texts, such as the modern gothic tales *The Woman in Black* and *The Mist in the Mirror* by Susan Hill or *Gormenghast*, by Mervyn Peake, are set in an indeterminate time-world. A third group of texts, such as *Wuthering Heights*, *Frankenstein* and Peter Ackroyd's *Hawksmoor*, veer between a narratorial present and related events from the past.

Note the emphasis upon the 'external' and subversive nature of the genre. Gothic, Punter suggests, lies at the very boundaries of the acceptable; hence it is linked with a historically remote time, or with the religiously suspect (witchcraft, the pagan, non-Protestant religion), the exotic and the foreign. Even where the action of the texts is firmly located in England, the location and action of the tales indicate the extent to which they represent values and demands that lie outside the bounds of the conventional and the acceptable. *Wuthering Heights*, for example, is set on the bleak and remote Yorkshire moors, whilst Susan Hill's *The Woman in Black* utilises the barren strangeness of the Eel Marsh to create its unholy and threatening atmosphere.

(2) 'Gothic works, it is often objected, are not fully achieved works: they are fragmentary, inconsistent, jagged.... If Gothic works "do not come out right", this is because they deal in psychological areas which themselves do not come out right, they deal in those structures of the mind which are compounded with repression rather than with the purified material to which realism claims access.... And it is here that we come to the crux of the matter: Gothic writers work – consciously or unconsciously – on the fringe of the acceptable, for it is on this borderland that fear resides. In the best works, the two sides of the border are grafted onto each other:' (David Punter, *The Literature of Terror*)

(3) 'Uncertainties about the nature of power, law, society, family and sexuality dominate Gothic fiction ... linked to wider threats of disintegration manifested most forcefully in political revolution.' (Fred Botting, *Gothic: The New Critical Idiom*, 1996)

(4) 'To make anything very terrible, obscurity seems in general to be necessary. When we know the full extent of any danger, when we can accustom our eyes to it, a great deal of the apprehension vanishes.' (Edmund Burke, *A Philosophical Enquiry into the Origin of Our Ideas of the Sublime and Beautiful*, 1757)

(5) 'The Gothic is a distorting lens, a magnifying lens; but the shapes which we see through it have nonetheless a reality which cannot be apprehended in any other way.' (David Punter, *The Literature of Terror*)

(6) 'Terror and Horror are so far opposite, that the first expands the soul and awakens the faculties to a higher degree of life; the other contracts, freezes and nearly annihilates them. I apprehend that neither Shakespeare nor Milton by their fictions, nor Mr Burke by his reasoning, anywhere looked to positive horror as a source of the sublime, though they all agree that terror is a very high one; and where lies the great difference between terror and horror, but in uncertainty and obscurity, that accompany the first, respecting the dreaded evil?' (Ann Radcliffe, From *On the Supernatural in Poetry*, 1816)

OTHER IDEAS

Thinking back to the idea of learning styles discussed in Chapter 2, you might like to think about how you can provide stimulus that is visual or auditory. Here are some ideas related to the study of Gothic and Classicism and the principles that underpin them, all of which can be related to the critical perspectives on Gothic above.

(1) Look at each of these images in Figure 5.2 and Figure 5.3. How do they capture the spirit of Gothic or its opposite, Classicism?

Figure 5.2 Examples of Gothic architecture

Figure 5.3 Examples of Classical architecture

(2) Use the Internet to find Goya's painting 'El sueño de la razon produce monstrous' (The Sleep of Reason Produces Monsters) and Caspar David Friedrich's painting Two Men Contemplating the Moon. What elements of gothic does each of these paintings encapsulate?

(3) Listen to the following pieces of music. The Gothic Symphony or Gargoyles – Havergal Brian; a classical symphony by Mozart or Haydn; Goyescas – Granados; a neoclassical piece like Stravinsky's Symphony in Three Movements. How does each relate to the critical comments and ideas above?

USING DIRECTED ACTIVITIES RELATED TO TEXTS (DARTS) TO PREPARE FOR LECTURES

These are activities that can very easily be devised to help structure your responses to a wide variety of issues within texts. You can use these to help yourself during your private study in a range of ways, or you could devise note-taking grids for use in lectures to help you organise your responses, using lecture outlines given by lecturers, rather than ending up with reams of long-hand notes which it will be much more difficult for you to decipher later. Below are some examples of DARTs activities that you might try using. Think carefully about the variety that they could bring to your individual study and how they could feed into your preparation for lectures, then do the activity that follows.

DARTS ACTIVITIES

- sequencing;
- tabulation;
- cloze – word-substitution exercises;
- prediction exercises;
- evidence-gathering activities;
- storyboarding;
- graphical responses – for example drawings, flow diagrams, venn diagrams.
- creative writing 'into' and 'out of' texts.

ACTIVITY 17

DARTs

Use the grid below to think about types of texts you might use these DARTs with and how using this type of activity could develop your engagement with your studies.

DART	Types of text	Learning benefits
Sequencing		
Tabulation		
Cloze		
Prediction		
Evidence gathering		
Storyboarding		
Graphical		
Creative writing		

In order to help you with this, here are a few examples for you to consider.

Example 1

Understanding the physical space of a text can be very helpful. In the case of *Frankenstein*, for example, it is important to understand the full extent of Frankenstein's pursuit of the monster if we are to appreciate the enormity of his emotions and the hardships he is facing. A simple outline map of Europe (see Figure 5.4) could be used to do this. Equally you could try drawing a setting or map of an area that is particularly significant within a text you are studying to gain a visual impression of it. What for example is the spatial relationship between the various locations in *Wuthering Heights*.

Figure 5.4 Mapping *Frankenstein*

Example 2

Language can be explored using DARTs. In this example, relating to Larkin's use of language in *High Windows* you could explore and keep a record of the appearance of certain types of language within the collection. This could be used to cover any aspect of language, though. Trains of imagery, for example, could be tracked, or the frequency with which certain words and their synonyms reappear within texts. This will also be useful as a means of gathering evidence in certain areas for assignments.

Precise and incisive description:	Qualified or qualifying, even tentative phrasing:
Colloquial, unpoetic language:	Intense, poetic diction and description:
Coarse and obscene language:	Sharp, dismissive diction:

Example 3

Thematic issues can also be addressed through DARTs. Here the prevalence of images of death in Larkin's *High Windows* is explored. The DART identifies a range of different ways in which death can be perceived in the collection and maps the appearance of these across the poems.

Poem	Physical death	Death of a place	Death of a way of life	Death of a personality	Death of hope
To the Sea					
Sympathy in White Major					
The Trees					
Livings I					
Livings II					
Livings III					
Forget What Did					

ACTIVITY 18

Developing your own DARTs

Why not try developing some DARTs of your own in relation to a text or module that you are studying? Think precisely about what your focus is.

Here is an example of a DARTs grid devised for taking notes in the Shakespeare lecture discussed on pp. 98–100. It shows how simple these can be, but also how effective they are in collecting useful evidence from the lecture. Preparing this kind of resource before going into lectures is invaluable. It means that you are already beginning to think in the terms of the lecture and allows you the opportunity in a structured way to make your initial responses to a text or topic. This way, when you go into the lecture you will not simply be reacting to ideas you are unprepared for, but will proactively be responding to whatever the lecturer says.

Questions	My thoughts (before lecture)	Key points	Examples	Issues to follow up
Why does Shakespeare matter?				
Is *The Merchant of Venice* a comedy?				
How important are the issues of trade and finance to the play?				
What does the play value?				
What is its view of 'aliens' and 'outsiders'?				
What is its view of love or of revenge?				
Other questions				

You could also use DARTs grids of this sort to gather critical responses to certain issues within texts or genres. You might, for example, take the key features of the Gothic and collect a set of critical and theoretical responses to it. Alternatively, you might take one particular critical stance and collect examples from a variety of Gothic texts and other secondary texts that exemplify or refute it.

NOTE-TAKING

Think carefully about how you are going to structure your note-taking. How can you most effectively balance the need to listen and participate in a lecture with the need to make a record of what happened for future reference? If you have devised some formats for note-taking, perhaps even partially completing these before you enter a lecture, using the module handbook as a guide, you are already well on the way to developing a set of well-structured notes as well as saving yourself time and worry in the lecture.

NOTE-TAKING INTO NOTE-MAKING

Once you have attended a lecture, clutching your scribbled notes in your hand, it is important that you do not leave the process there. Simply filing the notes you have taken during the lecture will not suffice. In several months' time when you need these notes to revise for an examination, or a year or so later when you may wish to refer to them for a dissertation, it is unlikely they will be very meaningful to you. Besides, they probably also contain references that need to be looked up and ideas that need to be developed further. As soon as you can manage after the lecture has finished you should turn the jottings you took in the lecture into an expanded and neat record, placing it in context with the rest of your studies. This way you maintain a developing sense of your progression in a particular module or sequence of modules and ensure that you have an effective and evolving record of your work.

SEQUENCES OF LECTURES

The above advice is particularly important when you are attending a sequence of lectures. Before the sequence of lectures even begins you would be advised to look closely at the Learning Outcomes for the module, so that you can plan efficiently for your studies. Activity 19 provides an opportunity to engage in this kind of thinking.

Ensuring that you return regularly to your lecture notes, seeing them as a work in process rather than a finalised piece of work is particularly important here, as you may need to revise or develop your notes in response to materials presented in earlier or later lectures. You may, for example, learn of an idea you wish to apply to the work of Shelley in a lecture on Byron. It is important that you do not see your learning in isolation, but draw meaningful connections within and across modules. For this reason keeping your notes electronically rather than in long-hand form is probably advisable.

ACTIVITY 19

Learning outcomes

Now look closely at the following Learning Outcomes for a first-year module on the Romantic poets:

Learning Outcomes.

After taking this course students will be able to:

- Define and understand the key critical approaches to 'Second Generation Romanticism'.
- Demonstrate a detailed appreciation of the poetry of Byron, Shelley and Keats.
- Develop their critical awareness of the following categories of poetry: lyric, epic, mock-epic, dramatic and the ode.
- Possess an applied understanding of the concept of 'the sublime'.
- Explore the ways the innovations associated with the first generation of Romantic poets (Blake, Wordsworth and Coleridge) are carried through into a new century.

What could you do before the module to prepare yourself for working towards these outcomes?

CONCLUSIONS

Learning all the skills of preparing for and working in lectures takes time, and at first the brave new world of the lecture theatre can be mystifying. If, however, you think carefully from the outset about how to prepare for your lectures, you will find the experience of attending them illuminating and even enjoyable. Remember that a lecture is not an isolated event, but rather is something that flows naturally from your preparatory independent studies and feeds forward into further reading and note-making.

6 Reading

By the end of this chapter you will have considered:

- the differences between reading at pre-university and at university;
- how to use your reading for a range of different purposes;
- the way to use reading as part of the study cycle;
- a range of strategies for managing the reading demands of your course, and how to plan for your reading;
- the role of literary theory in reading at university;
- two worked examples of how theory can be used in your studies;
- how to prepare for the theoretical demands of your course;
- a range of methods for recording your reading and the importance of doing so;
- reading for pleasure.

INTRODUCTION

Reading is not just about reading the primary text now. I understand now why people say they're reading for a degree – they're reading English – whereas before I used to wonder why did they say that. Because it's not just reading the primary text, it's reading all the other things that are around it. You know, the critics to see what they say, and the different perspectives on it. And it really does widen your knowledge of that book by getting lots of other views as well.

You will no doubt be familiar with the expression 'to read for a degree'. The expression does not come about by chance. Reading is something you will spend a lot of your time at university doing, especially in a subject like English Literature. For many students commencing their English Literature degrees, however, the volume of reading required often comes a shock after the comparatively light reading demands of A level, Access or IB courses, where you probably studied nine or ten set texts in great detail and with much less wider reading.

The study of English Literature at university is less about the study of set texts and more about the broader study of literature. Texts, of course, form the basis of study, but are covered much more rapidly, frequently at the rate of one per module per week. Occasionally major texts will be covered over a fortnight (e.g. *Hamlet* in a module on Shakespearean Tragedy, or *Frankenstein* in a module on The Gothic Novel), but this is the exception rather than the rule. There is, therefore, a considerable amount of material to cover. There is great pleasure to be gained from studying such a wide range of texts, but it does mean that teaching sessions deal with texts rather differently than you may be used to, and it is very important to keep up with reading.

As a student of English Literature you will be expected to read a wide range of primary texts, covering a variety of periods, genres, authors, national contexts and literary movements. You will also be required to undertake reading of literary journals, works of literary criticism, other contextual reading (e.g. history, religion, philosophy), online materials, module handbooks, and an array of other materials. Students of English Literature, in other words, use their reading to do a wide range of things:

- to prepare;
- to seek meaning;
- to contextualise;
- to explore;
- to challenge ideas;
- to compare;
- to analyse;
- to develop their writing and so on.

Reading can be the most pleasurable aspect of your studies, but it also needs to be carefully organised. The purpose of this chapter is to explore some practical issues you will face in coming to terms with the different reading demands your course will place on you.

READING AND THE STUDY CYCLE

Reading, like the other aspects of your studies, needs to be related to the study cycle outlined in Chapter 3. As you go through this chapter you should think about what types of reading you need to do at each stage in the study cycle in order most effectively to help yourself.

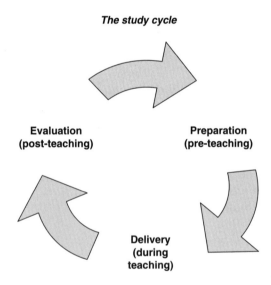

The study cycle

Evaluation
(post-teaching)

Preparation
(pre-teaching)

Delivery
(during
teaching)

- *Reading as preparation* – this includes reading in advance of primary texts for consideration, as well as theoretical texts. You should read carefully any guidance about teaching sessions given in your module handbooks and read around any general issues the lecturer has highlighted so that you are able to engage fully with the lecture or to participate in an informed way in seminar discussion. Such reading is intensive and will usually require extended periods of time, especially if you are reading novels, plays and long poems.

- *Reading during teaching* – swift, targeted reading during lectures and seminars. This will probably be reading set up by the lecturer and will consist of extracts of primary texts, theoretical texts and other texts the lecturer deems useful as contextual material for the lecture/discussion. You will be all the better prepared to engage with these materials if you have carefully undertaken your preparatory reading. You may also wish to suggest passages for comparison and discussion to extend, challenge or counter views emerging during the lecture or seminar, if you are given the opportunity and it is appropriate for you to do so. Your ability to be proactively involved in the shaping and development of teaching sessions in this way will again depend on the thoroughness of your preparatory work. There may also be the opportunity to raise any queries or difficulties you have, which you can only effectively do when you are thoroughly prepared.

- *Reading after teaching* – this may take a number of forms. You may need to return to the text and do some targeted re-reading in the light of issues that have emerged in lectures and seminars and which cause you to develop or reconsider your initial opinions. You may need to go away and follow up reading suggestions given by your lecturer during a lecture or seminar. You may wish to compare your learning in a particular session with what has gone before by re-reading and if necessary revising your notes.

READING IN ADVANCE

Reading in advance is a common feature of the study of English Literature both at A level, IB or Access and at university. You will soon notice how much more reading you are expected to do in the higher education context, though.

Obviously this is the reading you do to prepare for teaching sessions. As such it provides essential foundations for the work you will be doing in lectures, seminars or workshops. There are several specific benefits to be derived from attentive reading in advance. These can be summarised as follows:

- it prepares you for teaching sessions;
- it helps you to develop independent responses to the texts and other materials you are studying;
- it broadens your base of knowledge;
- it increases your ability and confidence to contribute in teaching sessions.

There is clearly, however, a difference between the nature and quantity of pre-reading required pre-university and at university. Figure 6.1 illustrates how often pre-reading is required at A level and at university.

In the experience of most A level, IB and Access students, responses indicate that pre-reading tends to be more limited in scope and is usually supported by materials to focus reading (for example DARTs – see Chapter 5). At university, on the other hand,

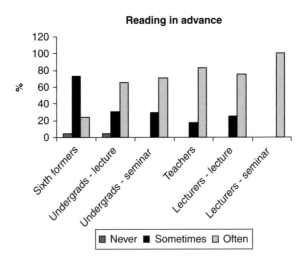

Figure 6.1   Reading in advance

Source: Green, A. (2005). *Four Perspectives on Transition: English Literature from Sixth Form to University*. Higher Education Academy English Subject Centre: Royal Holloway, University of London.

pre-reading is far more extensive and often without the specific guidance they received prior to university.

Finding ways to overcome this change is an important part of your move to university. As we explored in detail in Chapter 3, university lecturers often use module handbooks to indicate what they expect in the way of preparatory reading, and may well also provide additional guidance verbally in lectures and seminars. The ability to make appropriate and useful selections of reading for yourself is, however, an ability that your lecturers will rightly expect you to develop for yourself. It is part of your academic and personal progression.

This may at first be a slightly uncomfortable experience for you, and it is important that you spend time learning what your lecturers mean by reading and *how* they expect you to read as well as *what* they expect you to read and *how much* of it. Reading is a process, and the process at university is different from the process at A level, IB or Access.

> My A level didn't really make me read on my own – background reading, and so on – as the teachers told us all we needed to know. Therefore, reading around the texts was difficult at first – knowing the amount to do, and finding the time to do it.

The adjustments that you will need to make do not need to be frightening or overwhelming, though. Provided you manage your time sensibly, take a long-term view of the reading you have to do and learn appropriate processes for recording and responding to your reading, you are half way there.

CHANGING DEMANDS OF READING

The shift from the in-depth study of a narrow selection of texts over a long period of time (two years for A level and IB) to the study of many texts over a comparatively much shorter time period is the pleasure of an English Literature degree. Just think of it. Instead of having to make do with just a handful of great novels, plays and poetry, you will have the opportunity to enjoy reading and studying loads of them. And, if there are one or two that you happen not to like so much, you do not have to spend too long on them! On the other hand, this also brings its difficulties. One of the hardest things to come to terms with is managing the large quantities of reading demanded by English degree courses.

Study of literature at A level consisted of a limited number set texts over two years. University is more like a text for each unit each week or fortnight. At A level there was not enough attention to a wider range of literary issues and contexts.

The demands of reading will, of course, vary from one university to another and from one module to another. Figure 6.2 illustrates the kind of differences you may find between the weekly reading demands of A level, IB or Access studies and at degree level.

Looking at the column headings alone indicates something of the shift that occurs between pre-university and university study. The first two columns, dealing with A level, IB and Access, are strictly focused on set texts, whilst the following columns, covering four modules, are each focused on either a whole author's work (Shakespeare), a generic area of literature (Poetry and The Rise of the Novel) or a literary period (Middle English). It is clear that while contextual study may form part of the work that is done pre-university, once at university the role of context and contextualisation becomes much more pronounced. This is, of course, not to say that knowledge of context is ignored in the study of English Literature pre-university. You will know from your own studies that this is not the case. It is important, however, to realise that the place of the set text is very different pre-university than it is at degree level. Whilst at A level, IB or Access level the primary unit of study is 'the set text', at university the emphasis changes. Instead of spending a long time looking at one text and considering how it relates to the wider picture, you will now be expected to study the wider picture and explore how particular texts fit into it. In effect you are being asked to look at literature through the other end of the telescope.

A level/IB/Access			University		
The Tempest	*Regeneration*	Poetry	Middle English	Shakespeare	The Rise of the Novel
• Read Act 1 independently. • Close reading: prepare in detail Act 1, Scene 2, pp. ll. 1–180. • Read opening section of Act 1, Scene 2 as a class. • Read extract from critical introduction.	• Read Chapters 1–4. • Prepare in detail Chapters 1–2. • Read extracts in class as basis for discussion. • Read Rivers' paper 'The Repression of War Experience'.	• Read Seamus Heaney's collection *North* for lecture. • Prepare in detail a selection of ten poems for detailed seminar discussion. • Read background on The Troubles in Northern Ireland.	• Read 'The Wife of Bath's Prologue and Tale' and 'The Nun's Priest's Prologue and Tale' for lecture. • Prepare for group presentation on medieval views of women, using a range of historical sources.	• Reread *Othello* for this week's lecture. • Read *King Lear* for next week's lecture. • Read *Shame in Shakespeare*, Ewan Fernie, to compare presentation of shame in the two plays.	• Refamiliarise *The Italian* for lecture and seminar. • Read *The Monk* for next week's lecture. • Read Radcliffe's *On the Supernatural in Poetry* and Burke's *A Philosophical Enquiry into the Origin of Our Ideas of the Sublime and the Beautiful*.

Figure 6.2 A level/IB/Access and university – comparative weekly reading

Source: Green, A. (2007). A desk and a pile of books: Considering independent study. *Pedagogy*, 7 (3): 427–452.

Reading before meant just one text and drawing from it what you were supposed to, whereas here the text you're given is supposed to supplement the texts that surround it, if that makes any sense. That's your focus and then everything else supports it and holds it up.

ACTIVITY 20

Looking at reading

With these ideas in mind, look closely at Figure 6.2.

What differences do you notice between the amount of reading expected at each level?

How many different types of reading are required at A level/IB/Access?

How many different types of reading are required at degree level?

What are students at A level/IB/Access level using their reading to do?

What are students at degree level using their reading to do?

INTERPRETING READING LISTS

When you sit down and read through your module handbooks you will often be faced by long and intimidating reading lists. Your head will no doubt be full of questions as you read them. How do I make sense of this? Which texts is it essential that I read? Which should I read first? What am I looking for? All these are understandable and valid questions and it would be all too easy to bail out and decide to read Spark Notes instead. Clearly this is not an advisable option, as your lecturers are trying to help you and want you to use these reading lists to deepen and broaden your knowledge of the subject. You have a number of options open to you. First of all, of course, you should see whether you can answer them yourself. Lecturers will often guide you in one of a number of ways:

- sometimes reading lists are set out on a weekly basis, as in the example from the Shakespeare handbook discussed in

Chapter 5. This makes clear what texts you should be looking at week by week;

- sometimes lecturers will provide a section on general reading for the module and then will provide further information divided according to text so that it is clear how the reading list relates to a sequence of lectures and seminars;
- sometimes reading lists will indicate essential reading and will then provide further additional reading that you might do;
- sometimes texts will be presented in priority order, so that you can steadily work your way down the list;
- sometimes reading lists are presented in alphabetical order, but with brief comments on the books so that you can make informed decisions about what to read, as in the example from a course on Epic at Figure 6.3, where the lecturer has provided useful guidance on each text. Note that the lecturer has also provided the library catalogue number for each texts for ease of finding.

The comments in Figure 6.3 provide guidance about how to prioritise reading in a number of different ways:

- Auerbach – 'should be read by everybody' makes clear the centrality of this text;
- Blessington – points to a particular chapter and its content, but the caveat 'see Martindale's book (below) for a better study of this subject' makes clear that this is a generally less important book and should probably not be read first;
- Bolgan – related to a specific text covered on the course;
- Burrow – identifies that the book deals with 'epic development' and so is an important book for contextualising the study of epic;
- Davies and Wood – identifies that this is 'hard Theory', which is not necessarily a bad thing, but means it is probably not a good introductory read;
- Empson – a 'classic study' and therefore an important read;
- Hagin – the faint praise indicates that this is probably one to read at a later stage;
- Hatto – 'not a work that everyone is liable to find useful' speaks for itself, but particular passages of interest are specified.

Auerbach, *Mimesis: The Representation of Reality in Western Liter-ature* (trans. Willard Trask, Princeton: Princeton University Press, 1953). This is a classic; the first chapter in particular (on the role Homer played in inaugurating a particular Realist tradition) should be read by everybody. [828 AUE]

Blessington, Francis, *Paradise Lost and the Classical Epic* (London: Routledge, 1979). Useful volume, particularly the first chapter (on Satan as epic hero): but see Martindale's book for a better study of this subject. [825 MIL/B]

Bolgan, Anne, *What the Thunder Really Said* (Montreal: McGill-Queen's University Press, 1973). Despite the unutterably naff title, this has some interesting things to say on *The Waste Land* as 'neo-epic'. [828 ELI/B]

Burrow, Colin, *Epic Romance: Homer to Milton* (Oxford: Clarendon Press, 1993). Excellent account of epic development, especially the way romance elements of 'love and pity' infiltrate it. Well worth reading. [809.13 BUR]

Davies, Tony and Nigel Wood (eds), *The Waste Land* ('Theory in Prac-tice', Buckingham: Open University Press, 1994). Highfalutin 'hard Theory' readings of the poem. [828 ELI/W]

Empson, William, *Milton's God* (Cambridge: CUP, 1965). Classic study of Milton's epic. Readable and full of ideas, even today. [825 MIL/E]

Hagin, Peter, *The Epic Hero and the Decline of Heroic Poetry: A Study of the Neoclassical English Epic with Special Reference to Milton's 'Paradise Lost'* (Bern: Francke Verlag, 1964). Old fashioned, but still has its uses. [825 MIL/H]

Hatto, A. T. (ed.), *Traditions of Heroic and Epic Poetry* (2 vols: London: MHRA, 1980). More anthropology than literary criticism, and not a work that everybody is liable to find useful: but the outline of the historical circumstances out of which Homer came ('Ancient Greek' in vol. 1) and the lengthy 'Towards an Anatomy of Heroic and Epic Poetry' (in vol. 2) are actually quite interesting. [809.13 TRA]

Figure 6.3   Example reading list

If the reading list does not offer guidance in any of the above ways, or if you are in need of further information you can visit the library and look at the books themselves. The blurb and contents will give you some kind of indication about the contents and likely usefulness of the book. You can also, of course, share details about your reading with your peers and pick their brains about what they have found useful, or you could contact your lecturer – either in person or via email – to seek further guidance.

MANAGING YOUR READING

If you are to manage the reading demands of your course effectively, it is essential that you develop structured programmes for reading. In Chapter 3 we looked closely at how to develop a study timetable, and into this was built regular time for reading specifically attached to each of the modules. This is a very important principle. Time should be dedicated to reading in each module you are studying. As explained earlier, equal time does not have to be allotted to each module – it is just a fact of life that reading a big novel takes longer than reading a play or a collection of poetry – but nevertheless the novel, the poetry and the play must all be read if you are to keep up with the progression of your modules. To read one text at the expense of all others, therefore, will clearly leave you at a disadvantage, and you should make sure this does not happen.

As with most things, time and practice will make a difference. Once you have come to terms, for instance, with the style and concerns of a particular author or period, reading time will decrease. In addition, as time progresses, your abilities to scan and skim text and to read more rapidly will improve, making the demands of reading seem less onerous. An effective way to make sure you stay abreast of your reading is to make wise use of your vacations and any reading weeks you have. Request in advance the reading lists for the modules you will be taking the next term – even before you formally begin your course, most university departments will send you a recommended reading list – and set out your plan of action. There is no reason why you should not complete some, most or even all of the primary reading for your course before the modules even begin. This means that you will be well ahead of the game. You will then be able to undertake a structured process of re-reading to refresh your memory before lectures and seminars. This is clearly a good position to be in, as multiple readings of texts will deepen your familiarity with them and will also enrich your understanding.

> I think you should definitely have read the text at least once. It probably would have been better if I'd read them all over the summer then when I came back to university read them the week before as well. You really need to have read things at least twice before you can actually really understand them. And I'd ideally like to have done some of the secondary reading as well, probably in between readings so that I'd end up with different ways of thinking about the book when I read it again.

If this is not possible, it is important to set out a very definite schedule for reading, including time for re-reading. This may mean looking well in advance. If, for example, you are taking a course in the Victorian novel, you will probably be reading large novels by Dickens, Thackeray, Collins, Trollope, George Eliot and others. You will also, as has just been suggested, need to re-read the novels in the immediate run-up to lectures and seminars in order to refamiliarise yourself with them. In order to cover this amount of material you will need to think three or four weeks in advance about how you can manage this. Figure 6.4 illustrates the way this may work, imagining an eight-week module covering the work of Charles Dickens, Wilkie Collins and Anthony Trollope.

Planning your reading ahead in this way has a number of distinct advantages:

- it means that you will not be chasing your tail, desperately trying to keep up with reading in the run-up to lectures and seminars – remember this will not be the only module you are studying;
- it means you are building in time for multiple readings of texts;
- it means that you are systematically making time for critical and theoretical reading – this does not need to be done all at once, but can be spread across the whole module;

	Holiday week 1	Holiday week 2	Holiday week 3	Week 1	Week 2	Week 3	Week 4	Week 5	Week 6	Week 7	Week 8
Nicholas Nickelby (Dickens)	1st reading	Critical & theory reading	2nd reading								
The Last Chronicle of Barset (Trollope)		1st reading	Critical & theory reading	2nd reading							
The Moonstone (Collins)			1st reading	Critical & theory reading	2nd reading						
David Copperfield (Dickens)				1st reading	Critical & theory reading	2nd reading					

Figure 6.4 Managing reading across a module

	Holiday week 1	Holiday week 2	Holiday week 3	Week 1	Week 2	Week 3	Week 4	Week 5	Week 6	Week 7	Week 8
The Woman in White (Collins)					1st reading	Critical & theory reading	2nd reading				
Phineas Finn (Trollope)						1st reading	Critical & theory reading	2nd reading			
The Mystery of Edwin Drood (Dickens)							1st reading	Critical & theory reading	2nd reading		
Armadale (Collins)								1st reading	Critical & theory reading	2nd reading	Critical & theory reading

- critical and theoretical reading is never undertaken in a decontextualised way, but always happens alongside your reading of at least one of the primary texts you will be considering;
- once you are into the full cycle of reading (i.e. from Holiday week 3) you will be able to make useful comparisons between texts and authors as you read them.

By adopting such a planned approach to your reading you will be in the comfortable position of knowing that you are systematically progressing with your work. This may seem overly rigid, but it will also ensure that you continue to enjoy your reading. Unless you are carefully organised, you will soon find yourself on a treadmill of reading with which it is increasingly difficult to keep up, and this will mean that your reading becomes a chore rather than a pleasure, which would be a great shame.

The reading for one module will need to be set against the reading for all your other modules, using your weekly study plan, of course, to ensure that the reading for your other modules is also progressing steadily. Try out the following activity to set out a weekly reading plan for an eight-week term.

ACTIVITY 21

Planning your reading

Imagine you are taking the following modules and are required to read the following texts:

Recent and Contemporary Poetry – Seamus Heaney – Two weeks, Ted Hughes – two weeks, Sylvia Plath, Thom Gunn, Gillian Clarke, Andrew Motion

Modernism – *Heart of Darkness* (Conrad), *The Good Soldier* (Ford), *The Waste Land* (Eliot) – two weeks, *Ulysses* (Joyce) – two weeks, *Tarr* (Wyndham Lewis), *The Rainbow* (Lawrence)

Shakespearean Tragedy – *Titus Andronicus*, *Macbeth*, *King Lear*, *Othello*, *Hamlet* – two weeks, *Coriolanus*, *Timon of Athens*

➤

Medieval Literature – The Canterbury Tales (Chaucer) – two weeks, *The Parliament of Fowls* (Chaucer), *The Book of the Duchess* (Chaucer), *Piers Plowman* (Langland), *Pearl* (Anonymous), *Sir Gawain and the Green Knight* (Anonymous), *Confessio Amantis* (Gower)

Plan out a schedule for reading throughout the term, allowing time for first reading, critical and theoretical reading and second reading in each case.

Remember that you should look for ways in which you can make theory reading more generic. There are obvious connections, for example, in your theory reading for poetry, which appears in some way in all four modules.

RECORDING YOUR READING

When you're actually reading a text, you actually have to think about it at the same time. You have to start reading with a pen in your hand. It's just something you have to get used to.

When you are reading as much as you will be during your degree, it is important that you find efficient ways of recording your reading. As you read you should be looking to develop a set of notes about the text you are reading. You should be reading with a pen in your hand.

It is also important to realise that although your degree may be sectioned up into modules you should not allow your view of your reading to become limited by this structure. The reading you do for one module is not relevant to that module alone, but relates on many levels to all your other modules. It is not possible arbitrarily to divide nineteenth-century poetry from twentieth-century poetry, for instance. Your reading of one informs your understanding of the other. Similarly, a module taken on the rise of the novel will inform your reading of any other novels you study on your course. Literature is self-referential, and you should try to read in that spirit. Writers do not write in isolation, and you should see your reading in the same way. How much more exciting is the process of reading a book such as Susan Hill's *The Woman in Black*, for example, when you are able to identify the skill with which she uses source materials from Dickens's *Great Expectations*, Wilkie Collins's *The Woman in White*, and the ghostly tales of Henry James and M.R. James, and when you can identify the ways in which she plays with the gothic genre? Careful recording of your reading will allow you to keep a record of such useful and enlightening connections.

Below are some suggestions for things you should try to do in recording your reading:

- use DARTs – these are discussed more fully in Chapter 5 and can be used to help you organise your responses to particular aspects of texts you may be studying. Figure 6.5 shows how you could record the use Blake makes of the concept of love in *Songs of Innocence and of Experience*.
- Notes – you may wish to keep notes on a wide range of issues. Notes taken in the pre-teaching stage of your study will be provisional. They are your first response to the text, genre or period you are studying. As you have seen in Chapter 3, lecturers may well use module handbooks to give you pointers about what to read and study prior to teaching sessions, and if they do you should certainly make sure that these are explored. You may also wish to make summaries of key characters; write a plot synopsis; keep a record of major themes and concerns; identify major theoretical issues that seem to be of relevance; make note of any other areas of your studies this also seems relevant to; keep notes on form, style or language; useful quotations (with all reference details); and so on.
- Keep a reading log – this may seem like additional and unnecessary work, but take it from me, you will waste much more time racking your brains and fruitlessly searching for badly filed notes if you do not than you will spend making sure your reading is well logged from the start. It is worth keeping an up-to-date record of what have you read, when you read it and where your notes are filed. I would strongly recommend

Empathy/love for mankind	Divine love	Parent/child love	Romantic/ sexual love	Love of nature
	Introduction (*Innocence*)			
		A Dream		
		The Little Girl Lost	The Little Girl Lost	The Little Girl Lost
		The Little Girl Found	The Little Girl Found	The Little Girl Found
			The Blossom	The Blossom
	The Lamb			
	The Shepherd			
On Another's Sorrow	On Another's Sorrow	On Another's Sorrow		
				Spring

Figure 6.5 Love in *Songs of Innocence and Experience*

keeping an individual file for each module you study to avoid confusion. Within each file make sure your notes are indexed and that you keep a list of useful cross-references. It is very important to keep a careful check on where this information is for ease of reference at a later stage, when revising for examinations or preparing coursework.

• Keep notes of theoretical/critical reading separate from other reading. Theoretical reading is something that you will be expected to do throughout your English Literature degree, and in relation to a wide variety of texts, authors and issues. Of course, much of this reading will be initially related to a particular text or topic. It is important to realise, though, that it is useful generically across your studies, not only in relation to specific modules and/or texts. For this reason, I would advise keeping records of theoretical reading separate from notes on specific modules. This is not to say that you should not refer to theoretical issues in your regular module notes, but that you should supplement this with fuller notes which will be more generally applicable.

- Look for connections (e.g. if you are studying a postcolonial text such as J.M. Coetzee's novel *Foe*, you will be able to draw useful connections with other texts you might have studied, such as Daniel Defoe's *Robinson Crusoe* and with *The Tempest*, where Shakespeare deals with issues of colonialism; or, if you are studying the works of Angela Carter or Stephen King, you will find useful materials if you have previously studied the gothic novel).

READING FOR PLEASURE

Reading for pleasure is something we hear a lot about. It is the leisurely activity of reading clubs all over the country and is something in which you have no doubt taken a great deal of pleasure yourself. After all that you have read so far, however, the very idea that you might have time to read for pleasure may seem ridiculous. That is not, of course, to say that the reading you will be doing for your course will not be pleasurable. If you are careful about organising your reading as this chapter has suggested so far you should find the whole process of reading for your degree pleasurable and stimulating.

To be purely practical, however, not all modules and all books you study on your course will be equally to your taste. This does not mean that they are unimportant and deserve less of your reading time. On the contrary, where you find things less immediately appealing and easy to grasp you need to be more than ever concentrated and dedicated in your reading in order to overcome your difficulties. Nobody yet mastered *Ulysses* or *The Waste Land* at a first reading, and the pleasurable rewards of mastering your reading after plenty of hard work are immense. By the fact that you are studying English Literature, however, you presumably enjoy reading purely for the sake of reading, and for that reason it is important also to make time to read books that no lecturers or reading lists are telling you to read. Always try to have a book on the go which is just for you. And if you can not manage a book why not try the newspaper or Hello magazine. They will serve the same purpose.

READING LITERARY THEORY

The thought of using literary theory often fills students with dread. There are, it is true, certain difficulties that come with trying to apply theory to what may already be difficult texts. Robert Eaglestone, who has done much to advocate the use of theory, nonetheless acknowledges that there is a 'hardness' about theory that can seem off-putting. But there is also real satisfaction and excitement to be gained from the exercise of 'reading' texts with theory. Literary theory will form an important part of your work at university. For most students this comes as something of a new departure after their experiences of English Literature pre-university, where theory tends to be much less a part of the academic process. Figure 6.6 demonstrates this. Many pre-university students and teachers identify that theory and criticism are sometimes used in their teaching sessions. Undergraduates and lecturers, however, identify that literary theory is often a part of teaching sessions.

Pre-university study does to some extent address issues of theory. Assessment Objective 3, for example, requires students to 'explore connections and comparisons between different literary texts, informed by interpretations of other readers' and Assessment Objective 4 demands they 'demonstrate understanding of the significance and influence of the contexts in which literary texts are written and received'. Teachers' assumptions and expectations of what is required under Assessment Objectives 3 and 4, however, vary widely. In many cases the application of theoretical and critical material is minimal and can be mechanical, and as such does not straightforwardly prepare you for what you will experience at university, where theory is used much more extensively.

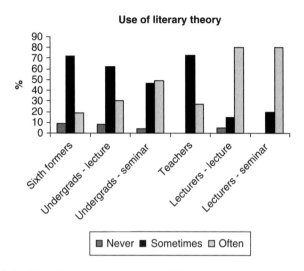

Figure 6.6 Use of literary theory and criticism

Source: Green, A. (2005). *Four Perspectives on Transition: English Literature from Sixth Form to University*. Higher Education Academy English Subject Centre: Royal Holloway, University of London.

So it is important to recognise that theoretical reading and the application of theory will be a central part of your work at university. The change in emphasis with regard to theory is effectively summed up by this first-year student:

> At A level theory was sort of the extra bit that was going to get you from a C to a B or an A. If you could find ways to go beyond the bit of text that was on your page. Theory was the bit that was going to get you the really high marks. Now at university those kind of things are implied – you're not going to get any marks if you don't look at theory, because ... the thing I used to view as being extra special is now mandatory.

You will quickly come to see the ways in which you can and should use your developing knowledge of literary theory. As suggested above, regular time should be made each week specifically for working on literary theory, and such reading should be undertaken in a different way to your reading of primary texts. Theory reading should always be undertaken in a context – in relation to a particular module or text. When working on Gothic, for example, you may well be prompted to read on the concept of the Uncanny and to read Freudian analyses of dream and sexual relations. You should never see such reading as related solely to individual modules or texts, however. Even if a theoretical paper you are reading is related specifically to an individual text (e.g. Gibson, A. 'Badiou and Beckett', in *Beckett and Philosophy*, ed. Richard Lane (London: Macmillan, 2002) or Eaglestone, R. 'Derrida and the Holocaust: A commentary on the Philosophy of Cinders', *Angelaki* 7.2 (2002), 27–38) you should read with an eye to its wider potential application in your studies. The above papers will help you in a number of ways:

- they will clearly provide you with new ways of reading the work of Samuel Beckett and holocaust literature;
- they will introduce you to some of the major ideas of the theorists Alain Badiou and Jacques Derrida, which you will be able to think about applying to a much wider range of the literature you are studying;
- they will demonstrate for you how theoretical ideas can be applied to literary texts;
- they will enable you to look closely at how effective writers about literature write about literature, giving you insight into issues of style, form and so on.

It will probably take you some time to come to terms with reading literary theory. Much of the theory you will be reading was not first written with the intention of application to literary study. It may be sociological (e.g. Pierre Bourdieu, Claude Levi-Strauss), medical (Sigmund Freud, Carl Jung, Jaccques Lacan), philosophical (Alain Badiou, Jacques Derrida) or political (Karl Marx), and as such may well conform to disciplinary codes with which you are unfamiliar. Many of the literary theoretical papers you read in journals or books may also be unfamiliar in form – the academic paper is, after all, a genre of its own – and will take you some time to learn. As indicated earlier, however, the satisfaction of learning to master new types of reading is immense. Spend the time and you will soon begin to reap the advantages.

To begin with it is probably best not to launch straight into 'hard' theory, but to begin your reading in one of the introductions to literary theory recommended in the reading list in Appendix 3. These books will provide you with an overview of the key issues arising from a range of literary theories. If you use the time before the beginning of your course to familiarise yourself with these, the reading of theory when you actually begin your course will not come as the surprise it does to many new students. It will set you on the road to learning how to read and think with theory.

The reading of literary theory and its relationship to your other reading can be thought of in two distinct ways, summarised in Figures 6.7 and 6.8:

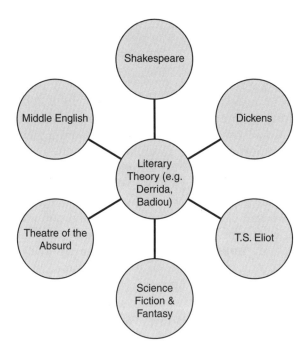

Figure 6.7 Theory 'out' reading

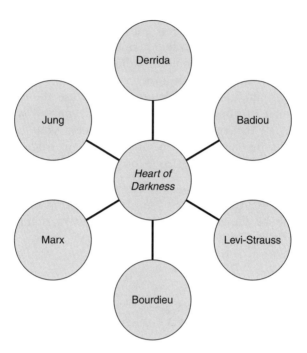

Figure 6.8   Theory 'in' reading

Each of these models for reading theory is helpful and brings its own advantages. The first, the Theory 'out' model allows you to take one particular theorist or a school of theory (e.g. deconstruction or postmodernism) and to apply this out to a range of the texts, periods and issues you are studying. The second, the Theory 'in' model allows you to explore a particular text or issue from a plurality of theoretical perspectives. In each case the type of reading you do will differ, but each will cast its own light on your studies. Of course, both types of theoretical reading are important. One complements the other, allowing you to use theory both to deepen your abilities as a close reader of text and also to broaden your perspectives as a student of literature.

RESPONDING TO THEORY

So what should be the role of literary theory within your studies? At the most basic level it might mean being able to respond with intelligence and in an appropriate fashion to the responses of your peers and lecturers. In itself this is a theoretical proposition underpinning reader-response theory, which sees the reader and the text as equal participants in the construction of meaning. The meaning of a text, therefore, involves acts of creative projection on behalf of both the author and the reader and meaning becomes conditional – a unique construction for every reader which is differently reconstructed with every subsequent reading. Without an active discussion of the processes by which individual readers employ a range of experiences to interrogate the text and build meaning from it, though, this is theory tacitly present but without explicit intellectual meaning.

THE TOOLS OF THE TRADE

To restrict 'interpretations by other readers' to readers only within your own classroom, however, would deny you the excitement and stimulation of exploring a whole range of readings and perspectives outside your immediate experience. Your abilities as students of literature and your enjoyment of the processes of reading will be considerably enhanced by some engagement with literary criticism and literary theory.

Although detailed knowledge of the full range of literary theories – reader-response theory, deconstruction, queer theory, feminism, Marxist theory, post-structuralism, semiotics and so on – is not immediately necessary, some understanding of the main ideas and perspectives of the major literary theories will provide you with the tools to view texts from a much wider range of perspectives, allowing you to develop responses which are both informed and independent.

WORKING WITH LITERARY THEORY

So, how might this look in practice? What follow are two worked examples to show how the basic ideas of some of the main literary theories might illuminate or deepen your abilities as a reader and the ways you can begin to think about texts.

EXAMPLE I: *FRANKENSTEIN* BY MARY SHELLEY

Here is a worked example based on Frankenstein. It looks at Freudian, Marxian and feminist ideas as a means of reading the text at a basic level.

Sigmund Freud (1856–1939)

Sigmund Freud, the famous psychoanalyst, formulated his theories in a series of books, *The Interpretation of Dreams* being the most well known. His work led to many interesting developments in the literary world, including the rise of the psychoanalytic school of literary criticism which has been highly influential. He is most famous for propounding the concept of the 'Oedipus Complex' (an innate sexual attraction to the parent of the opposite gender), the death wish, a focus upon the phallus as symbol and its corollary, penis envy, as well as the formulation of the divisions within the human psyche, which he termed 'id', 'ego' and 'superego'.

His ideas and their appearance within Freudian literary criticism relate in detail to the fictional world of *Frankenstein*.

(1) His concentration on infancy as the basis for subsequent psychological development is highly significant. The early portion of the novel focuses on the development of Frankenstein. Considerable significance is attached to the loving home environment within which he grows up and his father's notable failure to explain clearly to his son the reasons for his disapproval of the young Frankenstein's scientific research. Shelley also presents the reader, in Justine Moritz and Elizabeth Lavenza, with orphaned children. The monster is another significant example of this; Frankenstein, who stands *in loco parentis* to the monster, singularly fails in his parental duties of nurture and affection, leading to his passionate desire for revenge and the devastating events of the novel. Childhood is also significant through Shelley's portrayal of William, the first innocent victim of the monster, and the other children who, even in their innocence, reject the monster early in his life.

(2) Freud also believed that sexuality, repressed or otherwise, lies at root of human behaviour. In *Frankenstein* considerable emphasis

is placed on the idea of 'consummation'; Frankenstein speaks of the creation of the monster as the consummation of his dreams, strikingly avoiding sexual intercourse by creating rather than begetting a 'child'; later, fearing the results of a consummated relationship between the monster and any female companion he might create, he makes his fatal decision to renege on his promise to the monster; also, Frankenstein's marriage to Elizabeth remains strikingly unconsummated, the bizarre consummation of death between the monster and Elizabeth taking the place of marital sexual union. Shelley creates a significant sexual triangle between Frankenstein, the monster and Elizabeth.

(3) Emphasis on the oedipal relationship between parents and children is at the heart of Freud's theory and also relates significantly to *Frankenstein*. Shortly after he has succeeded in bringing his monster to life, Frankenstein suffers from a nightmare in which the figures of his mother and Elizabeth become entwined. Also, it is significant that the marriage between Frankenstein and Elizabeth is hastened as the dearest wish of the dead mother, as if she and not the love of the two young people is the driving force in the relationship.

(4) The psychology of the divided self is a further crucial element in Freud's theory. He identifies a three-way division of the human psyche into the 'id' (appetite-driven desires), the 'ego' (conscious sense of 'self' and awareness of others) and the 'super-ego' (sense of morality, sometimes seen as conscience). In *Frankenstein*, Shelley fascinatingly pursues the development of the monster through the stages of his development, and Freud's divisions illuminate the reading of the creature's growth towards understanding and revenge. She also significantly presents the divided and deeply flawed nature of Frankenstein through use of the device of the doppelgänger; in this device, the reader can almost perceive an externalisation of the warring elements of the human mind.

(5) Freud also saw the death-wish as a powerful psychological drive, based on a continuing desire to return to the womb. This can be linked to Gothic's frequent use of dark, enclosed spaces. The garret where Frankenstein creates the monster, for example, is like a nightmarish womb. Frankenstein and the monster are locked

in a pursuit to the death, and at times both express a wish that their sufferings could be ended by death (the monster's final desire is for self-destruction, and Frankenstein repeatedly refers to his own death).

Karl Marx (1818–1883)

Karl Marx is best known for his great work *Das Kapital*, in which, with Friedrich Engels, he launched an outspoken attack on the capitalist system. His concept of 'historical materialism' has been highly influential in the Marxist school of literary criticism; this school seeks to understand literature as a form of material production that participates in and illuminates the processes of history.

The following concepts are particularly applicable to *Frankenstein*.

(1) There are many perceived social or political 'messages' within *Frankenstein*. The novel clearly poses questions with regard to the social implications of science; it also delivers forceful messages on social inclusion and exclusion and the potential consequences of this.

(2) The particular historical and sociological period of the writing of the novel can be linked to key Marxist concept of the class struggle. *Frankenstein*, first published in 1818, was written against the backdrop of European revolution; the monster can be seen as a symbol of the destructive forces of social and political revolution.

(3) The reader also needs to consider how plot, characters and settings reflect the concept of the class struggle, either by inclusion or by omission. *Frankenstein* gives a symbolic status to both Franken-stein and the monster, allowing for a wide variety of readings in terms of the relationship between the powerful and the power-less. Shelley also makes extensive use of 'wilderness' settings, the harshness of which reflect the harshness of the monster's life and the brutality of the struggle between the creature and his creator. Shelley's use of a wide range of European locations serves to

emphasise the universal nature of the dangers signalled within the novel.

(4) A final key concept here is the way that, through class struggle, characters become 'outsider' figures and alienated from society. The novel is full of such characters. Frankenstein and the monster both become social outcasts and misfits; similarly the de Laceys, Safie and her father are victims of society's rejection. Justine Moritz and Elizabeth Lavenza are also social 'misfits' in that both are orphans.

Feminism

Feminism is a modern tradition of literary criticism and polemic devoted to the defence of women's writing or of fictional characters against the condescension of a predominantly male literary establishment. Significantly, in the case of Mary Shelley, one of the earliest propounders of the feminist cause was Mary Wollsonecraft, her mother.

A number of ideas central to the feminist point of view are highly relevant to *Frankenstein*.

(1) The relative silence and passivity of female characters in Gothic texts has been noted by many critics. *Frankenstein* challenges many of the typical perceptions of women in Gothic; the women in the novel are no more helpless in the face of the monster than men; Frankenstein's mother, Elizabeth, Safie and Justine, in particular, are all notable for their strength of character.

(2) The stereotyping of female characters according to male fantasy is a criticism levelled at a wide range of texts. In *Frankenstein*, Safie and Elizabeth and Agatha de Lacey are all presented as types of idealised female beauty and devotion.

(3) The concerns and plight of women are dealt with in a number of Gothic texts. Frankenstein clearly perceives Elizabeth almost as a possession and as his by right. The text also highlights the position of women under Islam, through its presentation of Safie. Even though many of the women in the novel are strong

characters, they are still largely obliged to live under the protection of males.

(4) As a text by a woman about the position of women in society, and women under threat, the novel explores the interesting relationship between the female author and her text, raising questions not only of male fantasy, but also of female fantasy.

EXAMPLE 2: 'DO NOT GO GENTLE INTO THAT GOOD NIGHT' BY DYLAN THOMAS

This exploration of Dylan Thomas's well-known poem, which can be found by a simple Google search, looks in more detail at how a range of theories might be employed in reading.

First of all, the poem may be considered from a range of perspectives – the text can be subjected to linguistic, literary or cultural analysis. This represents three modes of English study – language, literature and cultural studies – each of which provides interesting points of view from which to analyse the text. Some key issues for consideration in each area could be the following:

- *Linguistic* 'Do not go' is a negative imperative form of the verb; 'gentle' is an adverb (more typically 'gently') or may be a noun (a contraction of gentleman – in this case the poet's father); 'into' is a preposition of motion; 'that good night' is a noun phrase.
- *Literary* Adopts the artfully repetitive form of the villanelle, a circular French form; adopts a euphemistic approach to death ('that good night'); defies conventional peaceful literary death scenes.
- *Cultural* 'Do not go' echoes the biblical prohibition of 'thou shalt not' which is found in the Ten Commandments – reflects Welsh chapel culture; cultural fear of death.

Each of these perspectives provides issues for analysis which overlap and interact, and which should be synthesised in analysing the poem's possible meanings. You may, for example, connect the use of the negative imperative 'Do not go' with cultural notions of sin and death within the Christian religion, thus linking linguistic and cultural analysis. Similarly, the poet's use of the literary device of euphemism ('that good night') can be connected with cultural attitudes towards death.

Even at this simple level, therefore, the 'theoretical' division of the analysis of text provides us with complex and layered means of reading. This can be enhanced, however, by considering a range of literary theoretical concepts, each of which can open up further layers of potential meaning.

TAKING THEORY FURTHER

Formalist and functionalist theorists often focus on 'defamiliarisation'. This is a means by which the familiar is made unfamiliar, often to striking effect. A good example of this relates to the poem's treatment of death. We often see death as an absolute power which it is impossible to resist. Thomas's insistent instruction to 'Rage, rage against the dying of the light' and other imprecations fiercely to combat death, however, challenge this view. By employing the traditional image of life as 'light' and death as 'darkness', Thomas establishes a familiar view of death, but at the same time undermines the view that death is an irresistible force. This also stands in contrast to traditional romantic presentations of death in poetry, where peaceful acceptance and passivity are often the norm. The 'rage' and fight he demands of his father contrasts to the traditional desire that the dying should be at peace, and demonstrates the extent of the poet's emotion, powerfully conveying his distress at the seemingly passive response of his father as he approaches death.

FATHER AND SON

Theorists may use psychology to approach Thomas's representation of death in the poem rather differently. They may relate this to the biographical situation of the poet, who uses this poem to reflect on the disconcertingly changed nature of his irascible father as he approaches death. They may, for example, address the comparative mental states of the dying father and the living son, considering how they respond to the imminent death the poem envisages. What we may ask has caused the father, unlike the 'wise men', the 'good men', the 'wild men' and the 'grave men' the son envisages, to be so uncharacteristically 'gentle' and unresistant in the face of death. The appeal to the father in the final stanza to 'Curse, bless, me now with your fierce tears, I pray' illustrates the dying man's unfamiliar mental attitude. This psychological change also has its impact on the son. It is clear that he would rather face the fierce 'curse' of the father than such unnatural quietness. The juxtaposition of the words 'curse' and 'bless' makes clear the psychological turmoil of the son, who would see a 'curse' as a blessing, being more true to the nature of the irascible father he has hitherto known.

THE THERAPEUTIC TEXT?

Within the psychoanalytical approach is one strand called *trans-actional analysis*. This would place particular emphasis on the therapeutic nature of the text, looking at how the writer establishes an emotional framework surrounding death within which readers can explore their own emotional response to the issue. It is possible, as suggested above, to read the poem as Thomas's exploration of his own mental state. To that extent the poem may be seen as therapeutic, even cathartic. It is a means by which the poet works out his own complex emotions to his father's mortality and how the manner of his passing relates to his life. The poem also provides a means by which we can explore our own responses to death, however. These responses may be placed within either humanist (emphasis on the state of 'men') or religious (Christian notions of 'light'/life and 'dark'/death) frames of reference. This encourages us to consider our own relation with the issue of mortality and the death of close relatives.

CHALLENGING THE UNIVERSAL

Rather differently, *Marxist, Cultural Materialist* and *New Histori-cist* theoretical approaches often display an inherent suspicion of notions of the 'natural' and the 'universal'. As such they may well concentrate on the idea of natural/unnatural relations between father and son or natural/unnatural responses to the imminent death of a loved one. Is it possible, they would ask, to establish what such natural and unnatural responses should be? Such theories would challenge the idea that there should be any universally accepted response in either of these situations. They would see in any response a particular politico-cultural construct, created in a unique moment by a unique combination of forces. They may, for example, look at Thomas's use of religious ideas and symbolism within the poem. Why, for example, does he place such emphasis on imagery of light and dark? And what is the significance of the apocalyptic elemental imagery (imagery related to the coming of the end of the world) he employs in this poem and elsewhere – for example, in 'In Country Sleep', 'Over Sir John's Hill' and 'Poem on his Birthday'? Such issues point clearly to Thomas's Welsh chapel background, illustrating the power this social milieu had on the formation of his ideas. They create for him a means of thinking and of producing his responses to death.

RAGING SILENCE

Structuralist critics look to analyse the world (and literary texts) as a complex system of inter-related parts. They consider how and where these elements overtly inter-relate and where they do not. Hence they may look not only at elements of the poem that correspond, but also at the gaps and silences of the poem and what they suggest. This is a strikingly noisy poem in many ways, full of raging and storming as a selection of its vocabulary demonstrates – 'burn', 'rave', 'rage', 'lightning', 'crying', 'sang'. It is also full of profound silences, however. The only voice we hear is that of the son. What we wonder about are the views of the dying father, who is not allowed a voice, and what are the reasons for his quietness in the face of death? He will, we remember, neither 'curse' nor 'bless' the son in the final stanza, but remains silent. There is also a certain irony underpinning the use of words in this poem, which are seen as ultimately powerless. For all the son's desperation and anger, and his attempts to use language to force out meaning – illustrated in the circular and insistent repetitions of the villanelle – his words, like those of the wise men in stanza two, 'forked no lightning', becoming merely rage. Perhaps the greatest wisdom lies not in words but in the silence of the father.

READING THE FEMININE

Related to this, *feminist* theorists may choose to question gender paradigms in the poem, looking at the balance between conventional views of masculinity (rationality, impersonal exterior, noise, activity, strength, etc.) and femininity (emotional, personal interior, quietness, passivity, etc.), considering how far these traits appear and mingle in the poem. The son urges displays of masculine strength, noise and activity in the face of death, whereas the father seems to eschew such masculine 'rage', preferring the more feminine traits of passivity, quietness and resignation. The disturbance and confusion the son feels faced with this is profound and moving, displaying his inability, to borrow from the story of Elijah, to hear the still small voice of calm in the storm that surrounds him.

FINAL THOUGHTS

As these readings suggest, the point of literary theory is not to deflect your attention from the text. Rather, it can offer you a series of lenses through which to experience it, opening it up to readings you could not have reached on your own, allowing you a deeper and more complex appreciation of the way the writer has used form, structure and language to create meaning. For these reasons, familiarising yourself with the basic tenets of a range of literary theories can only be beneficial to your studies. As the great German dramatist and theorist Bertolt Brecht writes,

> A man with one theory is lost. He needs several of them – or lots! He should stuff them in his pockets like newspapers.

The metaphor of cookery is perhaps useful here. Do not try to spend all your time mastering and religiously adhering to one particular theory or branch of theory. A dish seasoned only with salt, cumin or paprika is out of balance. A good cook knows how to balance ingredients in order to obtain the optimum flavour. Your view of learning and theory should be the same. Develop an understanding of a wide range of theories, so that you can employ them appropriately to enhance the 'flavour' of your reading and your writing. This will be far more effective than adopting a one size fits all approach.

Some of the advantages of reading literary theory are identified by this student, who recognises that the primary set text is only part of the wider picture of English Literature at university. Going back to the metaphor employed earlier, she has realised that at university you are looking at English Literature through the other end of the telescope:

> It's not just reading the primary text, it's reading all the other things that are around it. You know, the critics to see what they say, and the different perspectives on it. And it really does widen your knowledge of that book by getting lots of other views as well.

ACTIVITY 22

Reading literary theory

Buy or borrow one or more of the following books introducing you to the world of literary theory:

Barry, P. *Beginning Theory* (2nd ed.). (Manchester, New York: Manchester University Press, 2002).

Bennet, A. and Royle, N. *An Introduction to Literature, Criticism and Theory*. (Prentice Hall/Harvester Wheatshaft: Hemel Hempstead, 2004).

Rivkin, J. and Ryan, M. (eds), *Literary Theory: An Anthology* (2nd ed.). (Oxford: Blackwell, 2004).

Summarise the salient points of a number of the major theories presented.

Use the ideas you derive from them to reconsider your understanding of a selection of the texts you studied pre-university.

➤

> Do not look to use them to form responses to the texts in their entirety, but use them to draw out particular issues and ideas you find relevant.
>
> Try out a range of theories on each text and see what each one helps you to draw out that is unique.

LITERARY THEORY – WHERE TO BEGIN

You will come across many theorists in the course of your studies. What follows is a list of the major schools of theory, key figures and major works:

Marxism/Historicism

Eagleton, Terry. *Marxism and Literary Criticism*. London: Routledge, 1989.

Hamilton, Paul. *Historicism*. London: Routledge, 1996.

Williams, Raymond. *Marxism and Literature*. Oxford: OUP, 1983.

Feminism

Belsey, Catherine and Moore, Jane (eds), *The Feminist Reader: Essays in Gender and the Politics of Literary Criticism*. London: Macmillan, 1989.

Eagleton, Mary (ed.), *Feminist Literary Theory: A Reader*. Oxford: Blackwell, 1986.

Moi, Toril. *Sexual/Textual Politics*. London: Routledge, 2002.

Psychoanalysis

Wright, Elizabeth. *Psychoanalytic Criticism: Theory in Practice*. London: Methuen, 1984.

Zizek, Slavoj. *Looking Awry: An Introduction to Jacques Lacan through Popular Culture*. Cambridge, MA: MIT Press, 1993.

Formalism and Structuralism

Culler, Jonathan. *Saussure*. London: Fontana, 1990.

Hawkes, Terence. *Structuralism and Semiotics*. London: Methuen, 1977.

Jameson, Frederic. *The Prison House of Language: A Critical Account of Structuralism and Russian Formalism*. Princeton: Princeton University Press, 1973.

Tompkins, Jane P. (ed.), *Reader-Response Criticism: From Formalism to Post-Structuralism*. Baltimore: Johns Hopkins, 1980.

Robey, David (ed.), *Structuralism: An Introduction*. Oxford: Clarendon Press, 1979.

Deconstruction and Postmodernism

Culler, Jonathan. *On Deconstruction: Theory and Criticism After Structuralism*. London: Routledge, 1983.

Culler, Jonathen. *The Pursuit of Signs: Semiotics, Literature, Deconstruction*. London: Routledge, 1993.

Docherty, Thomas. *Postmodernism: A Reader*. London: Harvester Wheatsheaf, 1993.

Hutcheon, Linda. *The Politics of Postmodernism*. London: Routledge, 2002.

Norris, Christopher. *Deconstruction: Theory and Practice*. London: Routledge, 2002.

Postcolonialism

Ania Loomba. *Colonialism/Postcolonialism*. London: Routledge, 1998.

Ashcroft Bill et al. *The Post-Colonial Studies Reader*. London: Routledge, 1995.

Ashcroft Bill et al. *Key Concepts in Post-Colonial Studies*. London: Routledge, 1998.

Chrisman, Laura and Patrick Williams. *Colonial Discourse and Post-Colonial Theory: A Reader*. Hemel Hempstead: Harvester, 1993.

Hall, Stuart (ed.), *The Empire Strikes Back: Race and Racism in 70s Britain*. London: Hutchinson, 1982.

Said, Edward. *Culture and Imperialism*. London: Chatto & Windus, 1996.

Said, Edward. *Orientalism* (2nd ed.), London: Penguin, 1995.

CONCLUSIONS

Reading is one of the greatest pleasures, but can also be one of the greatest areas of difficulty as you begin your English Literature degree. By ensuring you are well prepared for your reading, both familiar and new (e.g. literary theory), the changes in reading from pre-university to university study can be pleasurable challenges rather than hardships.

Remember the following key points and you will be well on the way to succeeding:

- use your holidays and any reading weeks you have to do as much pre-reading of set texts and theory texts as possible;
- always make time for re-reading texts before lectures and seminars – second (and even third or fourth) readings will only deepen your familiarity with the material you will be covering;
- make dedicated time for secondary and other theoretical reading;
- be aware that theoretical reading is useful across all modules you are studying and does not solely relate to individual set texts you may be covering;
- record your reading thoroughly, as this will save you time in the long run and will make your recall more efficient;
- spend time to plan your reading ahead – draw up timetables of reading for all the modules you are studying, especially when long texts are involved;
- read with a pen in your hand;
- talk about your reading with your peers;
- think about ways in which you can help each other with reading (e.g. preparing digested reads – see Appendix 1);
- make time, if at all possible, for reading that is not prescribed by your course of study.

There are no guarantees, of course, but by adopting these principles you will give yourself the best opportunity of continuing to enjoy and getting the most out of your reading.

7 Writing

By the end of this chapter you will have considered a range of issues surrounding writing:

- who do you write for?
- exploratory writing and free writing;
- creative writing and transformative writing;
- assignment writing;
- developing writing skills and writing processes;
- use of literary terminology;
- referencing;
- plagiarism;
- assessment of writing.

INTRODUCTION

Writing, like reading, will demand a lot of your time at university. Here is what some well-known writers have to say about the process of writing.

(a) Fetch me a pen, I need to think. (Voltaire)

(b) There's nothing to writing. All you do is sit down at a typewriter and open a vein. (Walter Wellesley 'Red' Smith)

(c) A word is not the same with one writer as with another. One tears it from his guts. The other pulls it out of his overcoat pocket. (Charles Peguy)

(d) Writing became such a process of discovery that I couldn't wait to get to work in the morning: I wanted to know what I was going to say. (Sharon O'Brien)

➢

(e)   I'm not a very good writer, but I'm an excellent rewriter. (James Michener)

(f)   The wastebasket is a writer's best friend. (Isaac Bashevis Singer)

(g)   Easy reading is damn hard writing. (Nathaniel Hawthorne)

(h)   The difference between the right word and the almost right word is the difference between lightning and a lightning bug. (Mark Twain)

(i)   Proofread carefully to see if you any words out. (Anonymous)

(j)   Write down the thoughts of the moment. Those that come unsought for are commonly the most valuable. (Francis Bacon)

(k)   Every writer I know has trouble writing. (Joseph Heller)

(l)   When something can be read without effort, great effort has gone into its writing. (Enrique Jardiel Poncela)

(m)   Writing comes more easily if you have something to say. (Sholem Asch)

(n)   The only cure for writer's block is insomnia. (Merit Antares)

(o)   Write your first draft with your heart. Re-write with your head. (From the movie *Finding Forrester*)

(p)   How do I know what I think until I see what I say? (E. M. Forster)

ACTIVITY 23

What is writing about?

Consider each of the above quotations about writing.
What does each of them suggest about the activity of writing?
Which comes nearest to your own views of writing?

WHO DO YOU WRITE FOR?

Throughout your academic career so far you must have written hundreds, possibly even thousands of pieces of work. Many of them will have been short, some of them will have been long, and they will have been produced for a variety of purposes and people. Here is a list of the people you have probably most often written for:

- your teachers;
- examiners;
- yourselves;
- your parents;
- your peers;
- a variety of imagined audiences and so on.

ACTIVITY 24

Your writing to date

Think further about this list. Add any other people or groups of people for whom you have regularly written to the list.

Write down the kinds of writing that you have done for each.
Of these kinds of writing, which is your favourite and why?
How did your writing vary from one to another?
Which of these kinds of writing do you imagine will form a regular part of your writing at university?

BECOMING A BETTER WRITER

Presumably one of the reasons that you have opted to follow a degree in English Literature at university is that you wish to become a better writer. You may well discover, however, that comparatively little of the teaching you receive at university is targeted at your development in this area, and that your lecturers will make the following assumptions:

- that you are already an effective writer;
- that you will take active steps to teach yourself how to write within the context of academic English;

- that you will use your reading of secondary texts, such as literary theory and literary criticism to develop your own abilities as a writer.

Let us consider each of these assumptions in turn.

YOU ARE ALREADY AN EFFECTIVE WRITER

True, you will have demonstrated through your A level, IB or Access studies that you have a certain level of ability as a writer. However, the assumption that what constitutes effective writing in the context of your pre-university study automatically constitutes effective writing in the context of an English Literature degree does not necessarily hold. For a start, much of the writing you did pre-university will have been done specifically with a view to preparing you for examination, dealing with single texts or small numbers of texts under timed conditions – the most common form of written assessment at that level. Much of your writing at university, however, will be in the form of more extended coursework assignments dealing with a range of full texts and related theoretical materials. What you have been taught to do as a writer pre-university, in other words certainly relates to what you will be doing at university, but does not necessarily relate to it in a straightforward way. You may well have to spend some time thinking carefully about how you need to develop as a writer and about how such developments can be made.

YOU WILL TAKE ACTIVE STEPS TO TEACH YOURSELF HOW TO WRITE BETTER

The nature of university learning is, as we saw in Chapter 2 and Chapter 3, very much based on independence. Your lecturers will expect you to do much of the work on developing your writing yourself. They may well assume, given that you have achieved an advanced qualification in English of some description, that you should have sufficient mastery of written English to do so. That

said, many universities now recognise that the nature o
at A level, IB and Access is different in a number of significant
ways from writing at degree level. To help their students develop
the necessary skills as academic writers (e.g. developing sustained
writing, dealing with increasingly complex concepts, using references) you may well find that you have the option to (or that
you are expected to) take a module or half module on academic
writing.

That said, the bulk of the responsibility for developing as a writer
lies with you, and it is important that you spend the time to do
so, as you will be expected to write a considerable amount in
the course of your degree. You need to be systematic in thinking
about what constitutes effective writing at degree level. Try the
following:

- ask to see examples of written work that your tutors consider
  to be good, or that illustrate competence at a variety of levels –
  sometimes bad examples can be as instructive as good ones;
- spend extended periods of time planning and preparing for your
  writing;
- talk about your writing with your peers – discuss points
  for consideration and test out the arguments you are going
  to use;
- use seminars as a place to pick up and develop ideas for your
  writing, where possible thinking early about the topic you will
  be writing on;
- make sure you leave ample time for proof-reading your work –
  maybe even ask your peers to do this too;
- make sure you read and re-read your own work, allowing
  time for redrafting so that you can refine your thoughts and
  arguments, develop your use of evidence and so on.

All of these steps will make a considerable difference to your out-
put as a writer. Below is a sequence for writing that you may
wish to adopt in order to develop effective practices as a writer
related to the cycle of study we have been using throughout the
book:

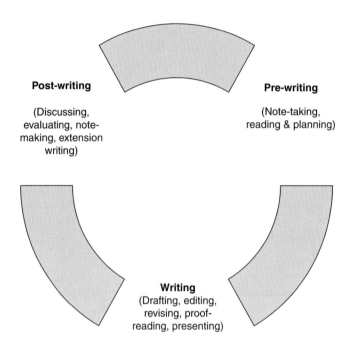

Post-writing

(Discussing, evaluating, note-making, extension writing)

Pre-writing

(Note-taking, reading & planning)

Writing
(Drafting, editing, revising, proof-reading, presenting)

Let us consider each of these stages in turn.

Pre-writing – any written assignment you have to undertake will arise from or at least relate to your work in lectures and seminars. The first stage of writing an assignment, therefore, is the notes you make in preparation for lectures and seminars and the notes you take during those teaching sessions. It is useful to familiarise yourself in advance with the assessment tasks and requirements of the modules you are studying so that you can proactively develop your note-making and note-taking to deal with this.

Your reading is also very important in the pre-writing stage of the process. Thinking carefully about what you need to read in order to fulfil the requirements of an assessment and to extend your understanding in the field is an essential part of the process. You should look to gather appropriate quotations and references for use in the written assignment, making full and accurate reference to where these are to be found – there is nothing more frustrating and time-consuming than having to trawl back through large tranches of reading in order to find a carelessly jotted-down reference.

Planning is also essential at the pre-writing stage. You should think very carefully about the content you wish to cover in written assignments, as well as the form and structure of what you wish to write. This is especially important when you are working to strict time limits and word-length requirements. This stage of the process may also include undertaking some exploratory writing in which you try out certain concepts and ideas to see whether or not they will appropriately fit into the bigger picture of your assignment.

Writing – Once you have undertaken the pre-writing tasks outlined above, the next stage is a sequence of drafting, editing and revising your writing. This can be a lengthy process, and may lead through a sequence of drafts as you compose, read and adapt your work. It is rare that the best exposition of your ideas comes out perfectly first time. Ask any writer. Writing is work and you need to allow yourself time to work at it properly. Ideally you should leave some time between finishing a draft and going back to read and revise it. Obviously the amount of time you can leave will vary, depending on how long you have to complete the written task. However, as you are writing you become very close to a piece of work and it is easy to become blinded to short-comings, inconsistencies and omissions. Time away from your work will help you to return to it with a fresh eye and will enable you to judge it in a more objectively critical way. An assignment may go through a sequence of drafts and redrafts before reaching its final form for submission. It is also important to do a final proof-reading and presentation check before submitting your work. Literal errors, weaknesses of expression, incorrect and incomplete references should all be weeded out and you should make sure that you have adhered to any presentational and referencing instructions provided by your department.

Here is an example of the instructions from a first-year module handbook where very precise details regarding presentation are provided. Lecturers will expect such guidelines to be followed to the letter:

Important – Coursework Presentation

You must follow these guidelines in every piece of coursework. Always ask your tutor if you are uncertain about any aspect of presentation or referencing.

1. For the main text of your essay use either Times New Roman or Arial or Helvetica *fonts*, in a *point size* of 10, 11 or 12.
2. Insert your *student number* as a header to the essay, so that it is visible at the top of each page (preferably the top-right). *Do not type your name anywhere on the essay*. Beneath your student number on the first page, include the following details, allowing one line for each: (i) your degree subject, (ii) module number and name, and (iii) module assessment number.
3. Copy out *the question exactly* as set. Put the question in bold print. Italics or underlining should only be used to indicate text titles included in the question – not for the whole question.
4. You must use 1.5 or double line *spacing* for the main text of your essay, leaving adequate margins (about 2.5 centimetres).
5. You should use a point size of 8 or 9 for *footnotes*, and these should be single spaced, not 1.5 or double spaced. The *bibliography* should be single spaced, with one line left between each text.
6. You should state your *word count* after the concluding paragraph (work that is found to be more than 10 per cent longer or shorter than the specified word requirement will be penalised), and insert *page numbers*, preferably at the foot of the page, in the centre.

Please print on *one side of the paper only*. Make sure that your pages are in the correct order.

You may at first think that such requirements are pedantic and pointless. However, your course is not solely about learning English Literature, it is also about learning good academic practices.

Post-writing – Once an assignment has been completed and returned it is important that you do not see this as the end of your engagement with it. Assessed assignments have important formative value for you and can significantly help you in your further development as a writer. Discussing your work with your peers and your lecturers can provide all kinds of insights into how work – both in terms of content and in terms of writing – can be improved. Evaluating your work against published criteria for assessment can also be very useful, as it will enable you to see which aspects of the assignment you addressed effectively in your lecturer's view and which you did not. Careful evaluation like this will enable you to think carefully about how to plan and execute future written assignments in the same or different fields of literature.

Comments on your work may indicate further avenues for consideration and/or further reading that you should undertake. This will help develop your understanding in the field and will assist with future writing on the topic as you read further and make notes to supplement the work you did in the original assignment. You may even wish to undertake some re-writing or extension writing in order to address the issues raised during assessment so that your written assignment more fully reflects your ongoing needs as a student. Comments may also relate to your style of writing or the ways in which you present information. Such comments are essential to your development as an effective writer about literature at degree level and should be taken seriously. Where you are unclear about what is meant, you should seek clarification from the person who has assessed your work so that you can develop these areas and implement the necessary changes in subsequent written work. It is important, in other words, that you think of yourself and your peers not only as producers but also as self-teachers of writing, working in partnership with your lecturers. The ultimate responsibility for your development as a writer lies with you. Thinking in a systematic and structured way about your writing will focus your mind on exploring the decisions that you make as a writer and will improve your abilities.

USING READING TO DEVELOP YOURSELF AS A WRITER

The relationship between reading and writing is not straightforward. The two processes clearly relate closely to one another. As speaking and listening share the medium of the spoken word, so reading and writing share the medium of the written word. But as a good listener is not necessarily a good speaker, so a good reader is not necessarily a good writer. The relationship between the two processes is complex. Gunther Kress (1986) describes reading and writing as functionally differentiated aspects of one process and adopts the metaphor of a coin. The obverse faces of the coin are integrally linked to one another, but face in different directions.

This said, however, the very fact that the processes of reading and writing are so closely linked means that you can use your reading to help yourself improve as a writer. You cannot, though, assume that just because you read (and you will be reading a lot, as we have already seen) you will automatically become a better writer. If you are truly going to improve your writing, you need to train yourself to read as a writer and to write as a reader. What does this mean?

Reading as a writer. This means that when you are reading you need to look for the ways in which writers working in a range of genres and writing for a range of purposes achieve their effects. You then need to consider how and when you could seek to incorporate these within your own writing. Needless to say, this emphasises again the need for you to make regular and sustained time for reading theoretical and critical materials, as it is in these that you will see academic writing about English Literature at work.

Writing as a reader. This means that whenever you write you need to think about how readers are likely to respond to what you have written. Is your writing fit for purpose? Is it clearly and logically structured? Does your writing convey the meaning you intend? Have you supported your thoughts with appropriate reference to the text(s) you are writing about? Have you clearly responded to the task, and have you guided your reader efficiently and convincingly through your work? Unless you ask yourself these questions throughout the process of composition (pre-writing $\Rightarrow$ writing $\Rightarrow$ post-writing) you will not be thinking effectively about your development as a writer.

It is very important while you are writing to spend time focussing on particular aspects of the writing process: planning, composing, revising, editing and redrafting. By spending time care-fully thinking about each of these stages of writing, you will maximise your potential to improve as a writer.

USE GROUP OR PAIRED STUDY TO IMPROVE YOUR WRITING

The thought of managing and thinking about all of these aspects of your writing alone may be somewhat intimidating. Naturally, much of your writing will be done alone, but there is an important place for talking about your writing with your peers. As recom-mended in Chapter 3, studying in pairs is a very important and useful practice to get into, and discussion of writing can and should be part of this. Making regular and structured time for this will have a number of benefits:

- structure helps you plan in a sustained way for improving yourself as a writer;
- it is very useful to see how other writers work and to talk about your experiences of writing;
- discussing writing with a trusted peer will provide a good context for constructive criticism;
- non-threatening collaboration;
- mutual sharing of ideas – though you must, of course, ensure that the writing retains personal integrity and is your own unaided work;
- peer-assessment of work will enhance confidence in writing, and will also help you to develop your self-assessment of writing.

The importance of developing your ability to think about your own writing cannot be over-emphasised. Thinking about your own thinking, or metacognition, is central in developing your pro-cesses as both reader and writer and form part of the study cycle introduced earlier. It will assist in a number of ways:

- spending structured time thinking about your thinking and the processes you employ in problem solving will help you to understand yourself as a learner – this is very important in the new learning environment of the university, where you will be left much more to your own resources;

- it will engage you in a critical examination of how you think and do things, which will in its turn lead to refine your processes as a worker and should lead to greater efficiency;
- deepening awareness of the processes and strategies you employ as a learner and the types of thought you tend to engage in will help you to improve the outcomes of your study;
- the conscious application of the procedures you learn to a variety of learning situations should assist you in developing more reflective and efficient learning practices.

As you become more efficient as a thinker about your learning you should aim to progress through a number of stages. These stages comprise a number of levels of awareness about your studies and about your writing in particular:

- make decisions without thinking about them (*tacit use*)
- conscious awareness of strategy or process (*aware use*)
- select the best strategies for solving a problem (*strategic use*)
- reflect on thinking before, during and after process, setting targets for improvement (*reflective use*)

CREATIVE WRITING

There are obvious benefits to involving yourself in texts through Creative Writing. By writing creatively 'into', 'out of' and 'parallel to' texts you can gain extensive insights into the choices authors make. By creatively adopting a writer's language you can engage in detail with issues of narrative, character, imagery, lexis and so on. Such creative engagement with text will involve you in deep critical and theorised reading, especially where the act of creation is accompanied by a reflective analysis upon the insights you gain.

This is not really surprising. The study of literature is centrally concerned with acts of creativity. Reading and the construction of meaning is essentially an act of creation or recreation, which can and should be explored in your own writing. The central importance of understanding and engaging in creative processes is outlined by Mikhail Bakhtin (1981, p. 280), who reflects on the nature of language as vehicle between addresser (author) and addressee (reader):

> every word is directed towards an answer and cannot escape the profound influence of the answering word that it anticipates.

He suggests here what he calls a dialogic relationship between the reader and the author and the text they share, a relationship in which the boundaries between author and reader are somewhat blurred. It is clear, then, that acts of creative or recreative response are at the heart of reading and developing understanding of texts. Creative Writing, therefore, has a central role to play in learning about English Literature. To opt out of creative dialogue with texts impoverishes the very act of reading. To prove the point, think about each of the following types of interaction with text:

- prediction;
- visually imagining (locations, places, people);
- referring back to previous events;
- empathic responses (laughter, tears, sighs, etc.);
- responding to what is not said;
- imagining what is not described;
- attributing emotions, motives and so on to characters/events.

Whenever you apply these strategies to your reading, you are not simply reading, you are also writing, either 'into', 'out of' or 'parallel to' the text you are reading. When, for example, we predict that Hamlet will or will not summon up the fortitude to kill Claudius (and it very little matters which we do predict), we mentally begin an act of writing that runs alongside and interacts with Shakespeare's. Again, when we visualise Mary Shelley's account of Frankenstein's creation of the monster, we use our own abilities as writerly readers to construct what he actually looks like. And when Cordelia receives her father King Lear's unwarranted rebukes in silence, we mentally write in all the things she does not say and store them away to help us read the events of the play as they unfold. No doubt you can think of many more examples from your own reading. By taking such responses to texts and formalising them within Creative Writing, where you can also experiment with the author's lexis, tone, form, imagery and so on, the benefits multiply.

Creative Writing and other creative approaches may have formed part of your experience at A level, IB and Access, but for many of you it will have been some time since you were actively engaged in Creative Writing. Creative Writing can contribute very usefully to your study of English Literature, and some of you may opt to follow Joint Honours programmes in English and Creative Writing, or to take Creative Writing option modules within your programmes. For these reasons it is well worth exploring how you can use it to good effect in your independent study, even if it is not directly required by your lecturers. Creative Writing and creative reading are obversely related processes, which can operate together in cementing stylistic, theoretical and conceptual grasp of text.

RESPONDING CREATIVELY TO TEXTS

You will probably spend much of your time at university writing critical and analytical responses to literary texts of varying kinds. Never underestimate the power and importance of being a creative writer yourself, though. After all, you are giving three years of your life to the fact that literature matters. And what better way to learn something about literature than to become a creator of literature yourself.

Writing yourself can be one of the greatest spurs to insight and understanding. You can gain things through the experience of writing 'into', 'out of' or 'parallel to' literary texts that you could never gain (or would at least take much longer to gain) through straightforward analysis. Apart from anything else, the act of writing creatively provides a very welcome alternative to the demands (pleasurable though these are) of analytical writing.

Creative engagement with texts, accompanied by deep thought about how these arise from and relate to the texts that stimulated them, provides structured personal opportunities to engage with literary ideas, effects and language.

Here are some examples from my own writing. Each of these was used in different ways to help me engage with my studies. The first poem, 'Larkinesque' was written as a means of exploring Larkin's poetic voice and verbal palette. Having read the collections up to and including *The Whitsun Weddings*, the writing was used to identify with his choices of imagery and the effects that can be achieved by relentlessly piling image against image in the attempt to build an impression of an absent persona.

Larkinesque

The future opens slowly, like an eye
In sunny dawn-light. Curtain-filtered
Flowers wilt on to the bed where I lie
In all the safe delusions of unwaking, quilted
In the miniature death of sleep.
I stir, feel the weight of bedding
On chest and lungs, an intimation
Of reality, a daily pall of weakness spreading
Through the body, a confirmation
Of the imprecisions of living. Fear creeps
Into focus as the eye accustoms again
To the well-known contours of the room,
Last night's random pile of clothes, the stained
Unpatterned carpet, a sparse, protecting womb.
Drops form on a glass where condensation weeps.

The following short sequence of poems was written to explore the technical demands of writing in the haiku form. The challenges of capturing very precise moments within the very strict 5-7-5 syllable form of these poems can only really be experienced by writing your own.

Four seasons

I

the crunch of a boot
snow moulds to the patterned sole
a frozen white foot

II

snow and ice release
life bubbles in the new earth
green shoots nose the air

III

desiccated skies
air withers in sullen heat
birds hang luminous

IV

light drains skies close in
paths rustle with leaf-litter
the crunch of a boot

This final extract is part of a poem written whilst I was preparing to teach Susan Hill's short ghostly novel, *The Woman in Black*. It was written as an exploration of the eerie location of the Eel Marsh as well as to try to understand the deadly destructive emotions of the woman.

Noises at the Window

The causeway stretches, a taut vein across
the muddy face of the bay. Water sucks
invisible beneath the pitted skin,
the ancient remembering skin that masks
all time, records all loss. A lead, flaccid
sky hangs pendulous with rain; clouds purple
with weight of water tumble down and bulge

into the encroaching sea. Salt tears drop,
pock-mark the surface; a gentle sigh as
water meets water, soul meets soul, deep in
the heart of nowhere.
She stands alone at
the window, unseen, artesian eyes
boring through her pain, scouring the muddy
wilderness that is her home, her prison,
her torture-house, craving the love, the son
the merciless mud will never return.

The final example is a parody of the opening of Dan Brown's novel *Angels and Demons*. It demonstrates the ways that Creative Writing can enable you to explore elements of an author's style and the requirements of genre – in this case the thriller genre. Parody requires you to pick up on key stylistic and linguistic features and to consider how these operate.

Prologue

Leonard O'Vetra was an intelligent man. So, when his attacker pressed a white hot brand on to his chest, he was not surprised to smell burning. In fact, the one thing that did surprise him was how the man happened to have a white-hot brand handy in the middle of one of the most secure research labs in the world. I mean, it's not as if it's the kind of thing you can just slip into your pocket and carry around on the off chance that you'll need it. But even this interesting thought did not last long as pain shot through his body. The acrid smell of singed hair tickled his nostrils, then the sicklier smell of burning skin and flesh.

It was dark in the room and he could hardly make out the face of his attacker in the gloom. This became even more difficult when he began to pass out from the pain.

When he came round again, the man was still standing over him. '*La chiave!*' demanded the attacker's throaty voice. Apparently an Italian. Though the accent wasn't quite right. So perhaps only an Italian speaker. 'And the password?'

➤

Just in case his victim didn't understand this was spoken in English. Though why he shouldn't understand 'And the password' in Italian if he had understood '*La chiave*' was not clear.

The inconsistency apparently didn't bother the assailant. He was an impressively large man and he now applied his full bulk to the brand as he pressed down harder on the white-hot implement, forcing it deeper into O'Vetra's chest. 'Ouch!' said Leonard. He had always been taught as a child that exaggerated emotional responses should be avoided at all costs, especially where the infliction of pain was concerned. It only winds people up.

'Would you mind stopping that?'

'Tell me the password,' the attacker grunted.

'There is no password!' Leonard heard his voice as if it came from somewhere outside of himself. 'Passwords are precisely what there are none of. So, you see, this whole violence thing is pretty unnecessary.' He paused for dramatic effect. 'I can't tell you what you want to know, because you are asking for something that doesn't exist. So if you wouldn't mind just removing the branding iron, which is actually rather hot and painful, from my chest. I'm sure we can come to an adult solution to our problem.'

ACTIVITY 25

Creative Writing

Why not experiment with Creative Writing as a means of engaging with text yourself? You could use the summer before you begin your course to try writing 'into' or 'out of' or 'parallel to' some of the texts you studied at A level, IB or Access. You may wish to do this purely for the creative pleasure of writing. You may, however, wish to link your writing tasks more explicitly to literary understanding, as in the examples given above. If this is the case, set yourself a particular focus for the writing and then use this focus as a tool for evaluating your writing afterwards, asking yourself the following questions:

- How effectively does my writing relate to the original (in terms of style/form/imagery/etc. depending on the focus of the activity)?

- What did I need to understand about the original text in order to do this writing?
- What new things have I understood as a result of doing this writing?
- What would I do differently if I were to do the writing again?
- What have I learned from this writing that will help me to be a more effective reader?

PLAGIARISM AND COLLUSION

Plagiarism is the unacknowledged use of source material, and with the plethora of material now available electronically, this has become a serious issue within higher education. As problems surrounding plagiarism continue to grow, scrutiny of ICT use continues to develop. Unacknowledged use of material is, of course, cheating. Material must not simply be copied and reproduced without acknowledgement of its source. Web-based materials, in the same way as books or journal articles, remain the intellectual property of their author. It is essential, therefore, to ensure that all use of web-based resources is properly referenced. In the same way as reference to a print-based text will include details of author, title, publisher and date, so reference to web-based resources should include the same information.

Collusion is where two or more students work together to write an assessment, and inappropriately use identical source material. Even where there is no intention to deceive, if two or more students produce substantially similar material, they may be asked to demonstrate that they were not deliberately copying (i.e. plagiarising). Collaboration is permitted in some assessments, but be aware of what you are doing in these situations: arrange your own work so that, even where you are involved in formal group-work, you report things in your own way. Any student found to have submitted as their own work an assignment written entirely or in part by another person is guilty of plagiarism. If you have any doubt about a piece of coursework you are preparing, the best advice is to speak to your tutor about the best way to proceed.

REFERENCING

It is important that all references you make in your writing are fully and correctly identified to show where ideas and quotations have come from. This demonstrates your own fair academic practice and also assists your reader. Below are examples of how to reference texts in a bibliography or list of references:

Bibliography

Primary Texts
More, Thomas, Utopia, in: Greenblatt, Stephen, et al. (eds), *The Norton Anthology of English Literature*, Vol. 1 (8th ed.), New York, London: W. W. Norton & Co, 2006, pp. 521–590.
Shakespeare, William, *Julius Caesar* (Arden edition, third series, edited by David Daniell), London: Thomson, 2005.

Secondary Sources
Barry, Peter, *Beginning Theory* (2nd ed.), Manchester, New York: Manchester University Press, 2002.
Starn, Randolph, 'A Postmodern Renaissance?', *Renaissance Quarterly*, Vol. 60, No. 1 (Spring 2007), 1–24.

Web-based Sources
www.wwnorton.com/nael – Accessed: 21 October 2007.

You will note that all references identify author, title, date of publication and publication details. The web reference as well as identifying the year of publication also includes a precise access date. This is because, unlike most print-based resources, many web-based resources are subject to regular modification and alteration. The inclusion of an access date allows careful tracking of the reference and follow-up by the assessor if desired.

USING QUOTATIONS

It is also important that you think carefully about the processes for presenting quotations accurately within your writing. Here are some key guidelines:

- All quotations must be in quotation marks except where the quotation is inset (indented). Look carefully for guidance from your institution, but traditionally double inverted commas are used except for a quotation within a quotation, when single inverted commas should be used. Whichever method you employ, be consistent.
- Quotations of *more than three lines* should be inset and do not require quotation marks – the indentation indicates a quotation. Generally, if you quote at this length, you should engage in detailed analysis of the material.
- Quotations must correspond exactly with the original. If you insert words for clarity, these should be in square brackets. Any omitted words should be indicated by three dots: 'Friends, Romans...lend me your ears'. If you emphasise any words in a quotation by italics, bold or underlining not in the original, you must acknowledge this: 'If Faustus *will* repent' (my italics).
- Line-breaks in poetry (including blank verse) should be marked by means of an oblique symbol (/): 'Giving myself a voluntary wound / Here, in the thigh...', unless the quotation is indented, in which case it should be presented exactly as in the original text.
- Sources of quotations must be identified. If footnotes are used, the first footnote reference to a work should match the full bibliography reference (as above). See below for the footnote reference to this quotation: 'Man can only exist in the world by fashioning for himself a name and an object'.[1] For footnote references to the same work following without intervening references, write as follows: *Ibid*, p. 39. Further reference to a work which has already been fully referenced but which is not immediately preceding should be presented as follows: Barry, *Beginning Theory*, p. 172.

- If you paraphrase arguments, points and ideas which are not your own, you must indicate this to your reader by more than a footnote after the final sentence.
- Titles of books, plays, long poems, journals and other large texts should be italicised or, where not possible (e.g. in an exam), underlined, but not both; that is: *Utopia* or <u>Utopia</u>, but not <u>*Utopia*</u>. Titles of articles, chapters, short poems and short stories should be in regular type, and within inverted commas. This applies to titles only: for example, use italics for *Utopia* the text, but not for Utopia the place; for *Hamlet* the play, but not for Hamlet the character.
- The requirements in your institution may differ from this, but should be precisely spelled out for you either in module handbooks or in a general handbook.

USE OF LITERARY TERMINOLOGY

Developing familiarity with literary terminology is a process with which you will already to an extent be familiar from your study of English Literature at A level, IB or Access. Obviously, your lecturers will make use of a wide range of technical terminology, and you will be expected to develop your familiarity with such terms and employ them appropriately yourself. In order to assist with this, it is well worth investing in a good dictionary of literary terms. Here are some suggested books:

Baldick, C. *The Concise Oxford Dictionary of Literary Terms.* Oxford University Press, 2001.
Childs, Peter, and Roger Fowler, eds. *The Routledge Dictionary of Literary Terms.* New York: Routledge, 2005.
Cuddon, J. A. *The Penguin Dictionary of Literary Terms and Literary Theory.* London: Penguin Books, 1991.
Kennedy, X. J., Dana Gioia, and Mark Bauerlein. *The Longman Dictionary of Literary Terms: Vocabulary for the Informed Reader.* New York: Pearson/Longman, 2006.

The following online resources are also recommended:

http://www.english.cam.ac.uk/vclass/terms.htm
http://www.tnellen.com/cybereng/lit_terms/

There follows an activity designed to start you thinking about the use of literary terminology within your writing:

ACTIVITY 26

Use of literary terms

The following is a list of useful literary terms without definitions. Learning the correct meaning of these terms and how to use them is important. However, the thoughtless and unsubstantiated use of technical terms by either teachers or pupils is unhelpful. A careful and developed explanation of the effects the author achieves by using the identified technique is essential.

Think carefully about how you would seek to define each of these terms.

allegory, alliteration, allusion, alternating rhyme, antithesis, assonance, bathos, caesura, cliché, colloquial, connotation, contextuality, couplet, didactic, enjambment, end-stopped line, feminine rhyme, genre, hyperbole, imagery, internal rhyme, irony, juxtaposition, litotes, lyric poetry, metaphor, metre, onomatopoeia, oxymoron, paradox, pathetic fallacy, pathos, persona, personification, plurality, prosody, pun, quatrain, register, rhyme, rhythm, simile, stereotype, symbolism, synecdoche, theme, tone, triplet.

- Are there any other terms you would add to this list?
- Try to find examples of all of these from your own reading, and explain in each case why the authors' use of these techniques is significant.

CONCLUSIONS

Writing is a very important aspect of your English Literature degree at university. Like reading, it is something you will spend a lot of time doing, and so it is important that you find ways of varying your writing so that you can develop your abilities in a range of situations. If you are serious about developing yourself as a writer it will take discipline and time. But by adopting some or all of the methods suggested in this chapter it need not be a dull process. On the contrary, it can be extremely rewarding, fulfilling, and even – dare we say it? – enjoyable.

NOTE

1. Greenblatt, Stephen. *Renaissance Self-Fashioning*, Chicago, London: University of Chicago Press, 1980, p. 219.

8 Using ICT

By the end of this chapter you will have considered a range of issues surrounding the use of ICT:

- recommendations for the Web;
- using Virtual Learning Environments (VLEs);
- study materials on the VLE;
- submitting assignments electronically;
- electronic literary texts;
- referencing ICT texts;
- plagiarism;
- Web literacy.

INTRODUCTION

The nature and quantity of Information and Communications Technology (ICT) resources available to students is developing rapidly. Many manuscripts, primary texts, secondary texts, audio-visual resources, commentaries, academic journals and so on are readily available at the click of a mouse via the World Wide Web. Increasingly, lecturers are developing their reading lists to take account of these sources of information, which provide students with a wonderful opportunity to access a wide range of material on any and every topic.

With this opportunity, however, must come caution. Whilst most print-based resources such as books and academic journals are subject to some form of editorial and review procedure, many of the resources available via the World Wide Web are not. Unthinking reliance on such resources can, therefore, be problematic. It is important to make use of the opportunities the

Web offers, but due caution should always be applied to ensure that information is accurate. Always make sure you check out the accuracy and reliability of any Web-based resources you use. Often module leaders will develop Virtual Learning Environments (VLEs) which will include the most important and most reliable ICT materials. Materials on such VLEs have the advantage that the module leader has deemed them good as sources of information.

RECOMMENDATIONS FOR THE WEB

The following are all useful sources of information on reliably and responsibly using the Web:

- http://www.intute.ac.uk/artsandhumanities/english/ – a well-catalogued and user-friendly list of reliable and recommended websites. Here you will find links to a wide range of sites, all of which have been carefully vetted and are considered to provide useful resources for students working in the higher education context.
- The website of the English Subject Centre at http://www.english. heacademy.ac.uk/ provides a link to a website of the week and catalogues previous websites that have been featured. This provides a useful resource.
- Jstor is a huge online resource to which your institution should have subscribed. Check out its home page at http:// www.jstor.org/. Through this site you can gain access to a wide range of journal articles. These can be searched by discipline, title, author or subject, and will provide you with an easy means of access to many of the materials your lecturers refer to.
- Lexis Nexis. This is a popular searchable archive of content from newspapers, magazines, legal documents and other printed sources. Sometimes it is referred to simply as Lexis or Nexis. Find it at http://www.lexisnexis.co.uk/.
- Lion. Short for Literature Online, Lion is a large resource of poetry, prose and drama texts online. It also includes a

large body of literary criticism and a reference library. Go to http://lion.chadwyck.co.uk/marketing/index.jsp.

- Google Scholar provides a good starting point in searching for scholarly articles on a wide range of subjects. It includes dissertations and other otherwise unpublished materials, but provides an important critical discrimination. It can be found at http://scholar.google.co.uk/.
- Project Muse is an online database of over 200 journals available at http://muse.jhu.edu/.
- Annotated Bibliography of English Studies (ABES). This is a selective bibliography that provides a guide to the most significant material published in the field of literary studies each year. Records are categorised into literary periods, containing full bibliographic details, keywords and a detailed annotation with critical comments. See this at http://abe.informaworld.com/sabe/home.
- MLA. This is an international bibliography, providing a subject index of books and scholarly articles in the fields of Modern languages, literatures, folklore and linguistics. It holds the details of over two million texts. Details are available at http://collections.chadwyck.co.uk/marketing/home_mla.jsp.
- A final recommendation is the English Subject Centre booklet *The Best of the Web: Internet Resources for English*. This booklet is usefully organised within sections covering websites dealing with teaching and learning, useful organisations and others relating to specific literary periods, genres and also specific authors.

USING THE VLE

What's on a VLE?

Tutors' use of VLEs may be very varied. Some will use it simply as a repository for lecture notes. Others will use it as a means to provide supplementary information to assist with your further studies. Others will use it for a range of administrative, chat room, interactive learning and assessment functions. Here is a list of the kinds of materials you may find on a VLE:

- lecture notes;
- reading lists;
- suggested Web links;
- journal papers and other relevant readings;
- visual images related to the topic you are studying;
- sound and video files related to the topic you are studying;
- information boards;
- resources;
- assessment tools;
- quizzes;
- discussion forums and so on.

The extent and variety of the materials available on the VLE will, of course, depend upon your tutor and the extent of his or her familiarity and belief in VLEs as useful learning environments. Do not forget that technology is more intimidating for people who have not grown up with it. I cannot remember the first time I used a telephone, and therefore it is not technology and not intimidating for me. I can, however, distinctly remember the first time I tried to construct a VLE, and can remember how difficult I found it. Do not assume that your tutors will be as familiar with VLE technology as you are and as prepared to use it and see its advantages.

LECTURE NOTES ON THE VLE

It is important to think responsibly and practically about how lecture notes on the VLE can and should be used. Many lecturers now post their lectures on VLEs, but it is important to realise that using the VLE can never replace the experience of attending lectures and seminars. Whilst it may be tempting to have that extra hour in bed, to have another drink or to go shopping, thinking that you can always read the lecture on the VLE later, you will obviously miss out on all the benefits of face-to-face learning and the interactions with lecturers and peers that are at the heart of lectures, seminars and workshops. Whatever the many virtues

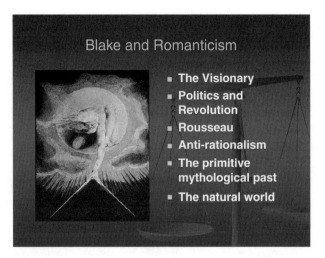

Figure 8.1 Blake and Romanticism

of ICT may be, it cannot interact with you and your learning needs nearly as effectively as real living and breathing human beings. Figure 8.1, for example, shows a slide from a lecture on the poetry of William Blake.

This slide provides some of the important information you may need as you begin to approach Blake's poetry, considering some of the ways in which his work relates to Romanticism. The amount of information it actually gives, however, is limited. It identifies headline ideas, such as 'anti-rationalism' and 'the primitive mythological past', but does not provide any information either about what these ideas actually mean, how they relate to and interact with each other, or on how they relate particularly to Blake and his work. The slide, in other words, provides a set of key points on which the lecturer expanded during the lecture. Similarly, the image included on the slide may be significant to the content of the slide and the ideas it refers to in a number of ways. These the lecturer may well have explained in detail, but that detail will be lost unless you attended the lecture.

The information provided is, therefore, of limited use to you if you have not attended the lecture – unless you intend to spend several hours by yourself trying to work out what it was that the lecturer

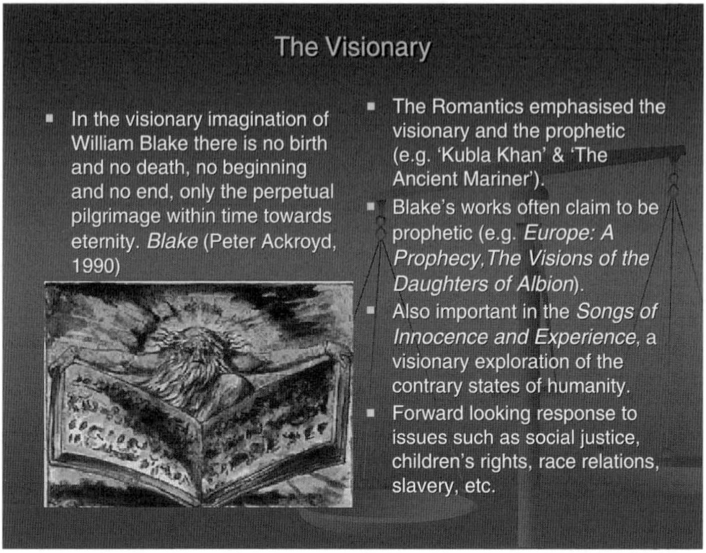

Figure 8.2   Blake – the visionary

said about these issues, and in that case, it would have been better to attend the lecture in the first place. If you did attend the lecture, however, this information will be both meaningful and useful as you return to the content of the lecture and think about developing the notes you took into a fuller set of notes for future reference and as you think about how to structure your independent study coming out of the lecture.

Figure 8.2 provides another useful example. On this slide there is slightly more guidance. The lecturer has included a number of things:

- a relevant quotation;
- a related image suggesting the relationship between a figure (divine? an image of the poet? a reader?) and the contents of a book;
- other related woks to consider – both by Coleridge in this case;

- relevant works by Blake that exemplify the issue of the visionary;
- a key Blakean concept – the idea of 'contraries', which is identified as a crucial issue in relation to Blake's best known work, *Songs of Innocence and of Experience*; and
- Blake's remarkable prescience as a social visionary.

Whilst there is more detail here, and fuller guidance is given about some avenues to pursue in seeking further information, it is still clear that this supports rather than replaces the lecture.

Questions abound as we begin to read this slide. In what ways, for instance, does Blake's unique brand of the visionary relate to the imaginary world of Coleridge? What are the philosophical ideas that underpin Peter Ackroyd's evaluation of Blake's visionary preoccupations? Are *Europe: A Prophecy* and *The Visions of the Daughters of Albion* simply titles that the lecturer used to illustrate the importance of prophecy and the visionary in Blake's work, or were these used as more extended worked examples? What are 'the contrary states of humanity' and why is this such an important idea in the *Songs of Innocence and of Experience*? What were Blake's views on the social issues identified, and how are these illustrated in his poetry? Again, much essential information is lost by failure to attend the original lecture, and much precious independent study time wasted, if the slide is seen as a substitute for the lecture, in trying to reconstruct the lecture rather than seeking to extend it.

STUDY MATERIALS ON THE VLE

Often lecturers will use the VLE as a means of providing additional information, posting academic papers and contextual information that will assist in your independent study and that will supplement lecture and seminar materials. Figure 8.3 provides an example from a first-year module. It provides contextual historical information relating to the work of the Augustan poets:

Historical Background

- *English Civil War.* The Civil Wars were fought from 1641 to 1649, when Charles I was decapitated. In the Interregnum, England was ruled by a reduced Parliament, and then by Oliver Cromwell (and his son Richard) as a quasi-monarchical Lord Protector.
- *Restoration.* Charles II was restored to the throne in 1661. Dryden wrote on that occasion: 'Oh times like those alone/By Fate reserv'd for Great *Augustus* Throne!/When the joint growth of Armes and Arts foreshew/The World a Monarch, and that Monarch *You*.' ('Astræa Redux')
- *Anglo-Dutch wars*: 1664–1666 and 1672–1673.
- Plague and *Fire of London*: 1666
- James II, a Catholic, prompted the *Exclusion Crisis* in 1678 (Whigs determined not to let James inherit the throne from his brother Charles; Tories are loyal to crown, and defend divine right of kings and passive obedience of subjects).
- *Glorious Revolution, 1688*: After Charles II's death, James flees to France; William of Orange accedes to throne. Has England become an elective monarchy?
- *Whigs and Tories.* Country programme to denounce political corruption and moral bankruptcy of Walpole regime.
- *Rise of capitalism.* Establishment of Bank of England. Stock markets, credit, risk, insurance, paper money.
- Reigns of Queen Anne (1701–1714), George I (1714–1727), and George II (1727–1760).
- *Jacobite Rebellion* (1715, 1745). Attempt by exiled Stuart family to return to English throne. Act of Settlement (1701) appointed the Hanoverian branch of the royal family lawful inheritors of the throne.

Figure 8.3   Study materials on The Augustans

Unlike the Blake lecture notes discussed above, these materials provide fuller factual information, though there is still plenty of room for individual or group study relating to these issues. The changing political situation over the period covered, for example, should be explored in relation to the poetry of the Augustans. Does the face of the poetry change to reflect the changing socio-political landscape? The materials presented on the VLE can be used to steer your own thoughts, providing information that is supplementary to both lectures and handbooks.

Other VLE materials will be explicitly designed to give direction in independent study. Below is a worked example from a VLE dealing with Old English poetry.

STUDY GUIDE ON OLD ENGLISH/ANGLO SAXON LITERATURE

A range of materials is included to help you with your independent study:

- it introduces key ideas about the oral tradition of Anglo-Saxon:

> Think of the difference between a pre-literate and a literate society, the importance of memory and oral transmission of remembered material from one generation to the next. The bard (the *scop*) was the walking embodiment of his people's culture and heritage: he memorised the ancient myths that explained how the king was descended from the gods; he knew all the mighty deeds of past heroes; he could recite the legal code; he could expound the intricacies of religious ritual; and, as important, he could perform to the accompaniment of the lyre heroic poems like 'Beowulf', 'The Battle of Maldon', 'The Wanderer' or 'The Seafarer'.

- it provides examples of the continuity of English verse drawing on the examples of Gerard Manley Hopkins and Ezra Pound:

> When Ezra Pound revolutionised modernist English poetry in the 1910s he decided 'to break the pentameter'. He did this by translating 'The Seafarer' into modern English. Find his version and look at how his poetry is different. Gerard Manley Hopkins and Basil Bunting both based their styles on Anglo-Saxon alliterative verse. Check out their works. What qualities do they share with Anglo-Saxon verse?

- it provides an activity relating to a film extract:

> Think of the film extract of Beowulf's killing of Grendel and reread the Norton extract of the event (pp. 47–51). Consider the contrast between the 'inner-yard' (feasts, warmth and apparent safety) and the 'outer-yard' (dark forests, tarns and bogs).

- it explores religious issues within the text:

> By the time 'Beowulf' was written down it had become Christianised (e.g. Grendel descends from Cain, the first murderer), but it was originally a pagan text. Is Grendel a memory of the old nature gods, the embodiment of the darkness and savagery of the 'outer-yard'? Think of Beowulf's heroic ethic? In what ways is his fatalistic view of destiny pre-Christian?

- it asks feminist theoretical questions of the text:

> Are heroic poems like 'Beowulf' boys' tales? Is there anything in them for the woman reader? What role do women have in 'Beowulf'? Is the poem's plot merely a matter of men boasting, fighting, feasting and dying?

- it offers ways in which 'Beowulf' can be related to twenty-first-century life:

> Beowulf is a superhuman hero, the defender of his people. Does such a figure only have relevance in a warrior society? Is there a place for the hero in modern society or are we all now anti-heroes? Are sportspeople the only modern heroes? What is the difference between being a hero and being a celebrity? What qualities in Beowulf would make him unfit for life in the twenty-first century?

ACTIVITY 27

Working with VLEs

Why not get hold of the texts referred to above and work through the suggested activities to see how they develop your understanding?

ELECTRONIC LITERARY TEXTS

Many texts are now available in a variety of electronic formats. Some of these will be generally available, others will be by subscription only. Many universities will have an institutional subscription to key databases, such as Early English Books Online (EEBO) in order to facilitate your use of these. Here is a selection of other useful examples of the kinds of resource available online:

- The Blake Archive provides access to a wide variety of Blake's works and also to a variety of editions of them, including accompanying illustrations. This is available at http://www.blakearchive.org/blake/.
- The Internet Shakespeare is a well-recognised resource, available at http://internetshakespeare.uvic.ca/index.html.
- Google Books is well worth a visit, providing access to a wide variety of texts, including many early texts. This can be found at http://books.google.com/.
- The Internet Archive provides access to a wide range of sources, textual and other. This is available at http://www.archive.org/details/texts.
- The Online Books page has links to a wide range of online texts. This is available at http://onlinebooks.library.upenn.edu/.
- The Designing Shakespeare database is another excellent online resource, bringing together photographic images of Shakespeare in performance from a wide range of sources. This is available at http://ahds.ac.uk/performingarts/collections/designing-shakespeare.htm.

- The University of Adelaide's site on the works of Charles Dickens is excellent and comes with online texts. This can be found at http://ebooks.adelaide.edu.au/d/dickens/charles/.
- Author society websites often also include resources that are very useful for students and some even have resources particularly produced for students. The Joseph Conrad Society, for example, does so. These are produced to high quality by recognised experts in the field of Conrad studies. See the resources available at http://www.josephconradsociety.org/student_resources.htm.

Figure 8.4 is an example of the kinds of study support material available, this one drawn from the Web pages of the Joseph Conrad

---

The Outer Station

What is signified by the 'boiler wallowing in the grass'?

What's implied by the statement that the blasting is 'objectless'?

What can we infer from the appearance of the chain gang? What attitude on the part of Marlow is conveyed by his referring to the man in charge of them as 'one of the reclaimed, the product of the new forces at work'?

What is the point of Marlow's disquisition on the various kinds of devils he's seen?

Be on the alert for where this motif gets picked up later on.

The 'grove of death.' What does Marlow encounter here? (What's the implication of the hole being as it is? of there being all these smashed imported drainage pipes? What's the condition of the people? What is Marlow's reaction? Should it/could it be anything else?)

The Company Accountant. What's striking about his appearance and behaviour? Do we detect any irony in Marlow's description of this personage?

What do we make of his attitude towards the sick person?

What do we make of his remarks about his laundry woman?

First mention of Mr. Kurtz: what expectations are aroused for Marlow by the Accountant's remarks?

Figure 8.4 Web resource on Conrad's *Heart of Darkness*

Society. You will notice the direction these resources provide for considering a range of aspects of the text.

Sites such as these are often the result of university or other academic projects and are, therefore, generally reliable, though care still needs to be taken. See the discussion of Web literacy below.

Much less reliable are texts that have been uploaded onto sites such as Project Gutenberg. It is important to be aware that just because something appears on the Web, it is not necessarily reliable and may not be accurate. Print texts are subject to rigorous editorial processes which cannot always be guaranteed with Web-based texts. It is, therefore, important to exercise due caution, as you may simply be reading the unsubstantiated views of somebody no more (and often less) well qualified than yourself. As a rule of thumb, if you are in doubt, check it out with your lecturer.

Reading Web-based texts can be difficult, and it is certainly a very different physical experience to reading a book. You will have your own preferences, of course, but should develop your skills as a user of both print- and Web-based texts. There are distinct skills attached to using both. Web-based texts, for example have search facilities that make retrieving information a very different process than when you are working with a print-based text, where different kinds of recording and indexing information will be necessary. There are also many things in terms of cutting and pasting materials that can be done easily with Web-based text that are very much more laborious processes with print-based texts. It is essential as suggested above, however, that you are sure the text you are working from is reliable and accurate.

REFERENCING ICT TEXTS

See Chapter 7, where the issue of referencing is explained.

PLAGIARISM

See Chapter 7, where the issue of plagiarism is explained.

WEB LITERACY

An excellent online Web literacy tutorial is available at the Penn University library's website: http://gethelp.library.upenn.edu/guides/tutorials/webliteracy/. I would strongly recommend that you take the time to do this online tutorial, which introduces you to a wealth of essential information about using and properly interrogating online sources. In general, bear in mind the following issues:

- *Authority* – find out who the author of the source is. What are his or her credentials in academic terms? Does it come with an academic imprint? Is it from a reliable source?
- *Accuracy* – check the basic facts and figures of the source out. If you discover inaccuracies and inconsistencies within the source or between this source and other reliable sources, then it is unlikely to be a good resource for you to use.
- *Bias* – is the information presented in the source referenced or does it simply make unsubstantiated claims? Does it present a balanced and fair view of the topic, or is it pushing an obvious and one-sided agenda?
- *Currency* – is the resource up to date? Check out when the page was last updated. You should always provide access dates for any web sources you employ.
- *Coverage* – does the source provide you with adequate detail and coverage in the area you need?

CONCLUSIONS

The world of academic English is slowly moving to take on board developments in the world of ICT. Sometimes – rare, but not unheard of – English departments in universities even run computer-based teaching sessions. It is also becoming more regular to find lecturers supporting students and extending structured input through the medium of a VLE. Such materials should be used carefully as a means of assisting in your independent studies. The World Wide Web also provides you with a wealth of materials to employ in your studies. The watchwords here, however, are responsibility and caution. Irresponsible practice does not assist you and may well end up in trouble – either because sources are unreliable or because you are engaging in malpractice. ICT provides a wonderful world of possibility where used with due caution.

9 Final thoughts

'If you think . . . that anything like a romance is preparing for you, reader, you were never more mistaken. Do you anticipate sentiment, and poetry, and reverie? Do you expect passion, and stimulus, and melodrama? Calm your expectations, reduce them to a lowly standard. Something real, cool and solid lies before you; something unromantic as Monday morning, when all who have work wake with the consciousness that they must rise and betake themselves thereto.'

Charlotte Bronte: Prelude to *Shirley*.

'What work I have done I have done because it has been play. If it had been work I shouldn't have done it. Who was it who said, "Blessed is the man who has found his work"? Whoever it was he had the right idea in his mind.'

Mark Twain: 'A Humorist's Confession'

'I'm a great believer in luck, and I find the harder I work the more I have of it.'

Thomas Carlyle: *Past and Present*

As you start your English Literature degree, which of these quotations most nearly reflects your view of the work you face over the next few years? The question is an important one, because hard work is certainly required on the road towards your degree. English Literature at university is not only clearly related to, but also distinctly different from English Literature at A level, Access or IB and you will have to work hard in order to bridge the gaps you discover. Making a successful start to your university studies depends upon recognising where and how the subject changes. It also depends upon learning how to operate within new learning environments and new expectations.

The process of coming to terms with the world of university English Literature can be managed effectively, though, and it is my hope that this book will help you do so. It has introduced you to precisely the areas where you may find difficulty as you begin your course, and it has suggested constructive ways in which you can begin thinking about them so that you can make the best possible start to your university career.

Whether you are reading or writing, working alone or in a pair, participating in a lecture or a seminar or a workshop, the study of English Literature is always fascinating. It may be hard work, in fact it may be very hard work, but there is immense satisfaction to be gained from struggling with difficulty and overcoming. The more you put in and the better prepared you are to participate, the greater your enjoyment will be. Following the guidelines in this book should help you to concentrate your mind as you learn to function in the new and exciting environment that is university and should make the transition into your time at university easier.

Wherever you are studying and whatever form your degree takes, enjoy your study of English Literature.

Appendix I   Ideas for paired and group study

This is by no means intended to be an exhaustive list of the possibilities available to you, but is intended as a list of ideas you might try to get you started in your group and/or paired study time. The key to successful group study is variety and creativity. The more imaginative you can be the better, and you will no doubt soon begin to develop many ideas of your own. In the meantime, try some of these.

MAPPING TEXTS

It is often useful to understand the physical space within which texts take place. When reading a novel such as *Frankenstein*, for example, which ranges widely across Europe and beyond, it is helpful to understand how far and wide Victor and the monster travel in their increasingly frantic pursuit of one another. By using a map visually to represent the movement of the characters, new understanding can be reached. Similarly, it can be useful to use the detailed descriptions authors provide of specific locations (e.g. the interior of Wuthering Heights in the novel of that name) to draw up a spatial representation. In studying drama texts, it can be very useful to draw up stage plans for key scenes to understand the dramatic possibilities of texts. Within the group context, try agreeing on a particular mapping activity, all draw up your own maps independently and then compare them. This can lead to lively discussion about the choices you have made and can lead into very useful wider discussion of the text and related issues.

STORYBOARDING

This is another method of visualising texts. Select one or more scenes or episodes from the texts you are studying and think carefully about how you would represent these moments or sequences visually. This can be very effective in enabling you to focus in on the key moments of texts. Within the group context, try agreeing on a particular moment or episode for storyboarding, all draw up your own storyboards independently and then compare them. This can lead to lively discussion about the choices you have made and can lead into very useful wider discussion of the text and related issues.

HOTSEATING

This is a drama activity with which you may well be familiar. It requires individuals within the group to take on a particular character from a text you are studying, say *Hamlet* or *David Copperfield*. The others in the group are responsible for asking questions of this character (or panel of characters). This will work best if time is given in advance for the 'actors' to prepare their characters and for the others to prepare their questions.

A variant on this may be for panellists to take on the role of particular literary theorists or critics or authors and to respond to questions of either a general or a text-specific nature. On a practical note, it is a good idea to appoint a chair so that the questioning and discussion can be effectively managed.

SPEED-DATING

Each member of a group prepares the key concepts of a chosen literary theorist, a personal response to particular issues in a set text and so on. Half the group remains static throughout this activity while the other half circulates. They will spend ten minutes at each 'date', when each member of the group will take a strict five minutes each explaining their particular point of view. They will spend a further ten minutes establishing the 'compatibility' or 'incompatibility' of their respective theories or perspectives. This is a good way of introducing a range of ideas into discussion and ensuring that everybody is actively involved. A further plenary discussion of the activity can then be used to explore any particularly interesting issues that have come up in the course of the activity.

GROUP CAROUSEL

This can be very useful if you are working in groups. Each bring along a particular critical, theoretical or literary text printed in the middle of an A3 sheet of paper. You circulate the room spending, say, five minutes at each text. In that time you are free to respond to it in any way you choose – you can write questions, make statements, provide examples from your reading, compare it to other texts or perspectives you may know, write creatively. As you move on you should feel free to respond not only to the original text, but also to the responses others have written to it. These sheets can then be used as a stimulus to debate and conversation, providing a sound structure for the study session.

ROLE PLAY

Role play activities can be used in a wide range of contexts to explore texts, both primary and secondary. Take on particular characters and explore characters' motivations and thoughts or other possible avenues of understanding. Such activities can be used in relation to drama texts, poetry or prose. It is often particularly useful to use role play to explore events that are alluded to but never actually seen within texts. You could, for example, use role play to explore what a particular character does between appearances within a text you are studying. It is also a very useful activity for thinking about the language characters and authors employ.

INNER CIRCLE, OUTER CIRCLE

A small group sits in an inner circle, while the rest sit in an outer circle. The inner circle are the active participants, while those in the outer circle are observers and note takers. Those in the inner circle may undertake a range of activities, such as role play, improvisation, debate, discussion. Those in the outer circle are responsible for making a record of the key points emerging from the work of those in the inner circle, or for offering feedback.

As a variant, you may wish to arrange for members of the outer circle to swap in and out of the inner circle for variety.

OPINION CHAINS

Each member of the group brings a particular opinion or statement on an agreed text or topic to the group study session. This may be a statement of their own, a theoretical proposition, or an extract of criticism (e.g. a newspaper review). These should be distributed around the room and then the members of the group circulate, writing their response to each opinion in turn. They can also respond to others' responses to the initial opinions. This can provide a very useful basis for discussion and can be very good activity to get discussion going.

NEWSNIGHT REVIEW

This is a very good activity for trying out your familiarity with literary texts, literary theory and analysis, and is also great fun. If you are not familiar with Newsnight Review, make a point of watching it on a Friday evening on BBC2. Take one of the texts you are focusing on for each module you are studying and make sure you are thoroughly familiar with them. You may also choose to allocate a particular theoretical or critical perspective to each participant on the panel. The panellists then discuss the text from their various perspectives, as in the Friday night Newsnight Review slot. To make the discussion flow and to ensure that everyone has their say, it would be worth appointing a chair, who will manage the discussion.

WRITING IN THE STYLE OF . . .

This does not have to be undertaken in groups, but may well be used by a study group as an activity to prompt discussion. The group will decide upon a particular author they wish to focus on. Together or individually they can then identify the particular stylistic features of this author's writings. They should then employ these in a piece of creative writing of their own. This could be either a completely new piece of writing or a piece of writing arising from a particular text.

As a variation, this activity could also be undertaken using particular critical or theoretical writers as models. This kind of activity which encourages a very close focus on the linguistic and cognitive world of the author under consideration can yield very useful insights into the creative and literary process, which can and should be discussed.

IMAGES

Each member of the group has to find and bring in an image or a number of images that they believe relate closely to the text or issues under consideration. These can be used as discussion starters.

CONTEXTS

Each member of the group is responsible for finding and bringing in one or more pieces of interesting, useful, or maybe even bizarre contextual information relating to the focus of study. These can be discussed in the group context as a way into the text or issue under consideration.

KWL GRIDS

These can be used before, during and after group study sessions. They are also very useful for working on your own in preparation for seminars and lectures, and in following up on them. They are simply a three-column table, as below:

K	W	L

In the left-hand column write down what (if anything) you already know about the text or topic under consideration. In the middle column write down what you want to know about it. In the right-hand column record what you learn about the issues you have identified in the left and middle columns. This will provide you with a useful record of your learning process and can be used as the basis for a fuller set of notes.

ZONES OF PROXIMITY

Gather together a number of pieces of contextual information about a text, or ten critical/theoretical views of it, each on separate pieces of paper. Give one set to each group member. Individually, place these pieces of information around the title of the text. The closer a piece of paper is to the title the more useful it is, the further away the less useful. Use these individual 'zones of proximity' as the basis for paired or group discussion.

As a variant, you may choose a particular critical or theoretical perspective as the centre point and place the titles of a range of texts around it following the same principle, according to how useful this particular perspective is as a means of reading the various texts.

TEXT TRANSFORMATIONS

Take an extract of text in one form or genre and transform it into another. For example, rewrite the opening section of *A Christmas*

Carol and transform it into a radio play script or a stage play. Or rewrite the opening scene of *Hamlet* as the first chapter of a novel. This will really help you focus on the demands of different genres and the ways in which they convey meaning (e.g. the use of sound effects in a radio play, or the use of descriptive writing in a novel, or the ways in which authors in different genres create character, sense of place or atmosphere). These pieces of transformative writing can be used as the basis for a discussion of writing process, considering what has been learned about the original text through the act of transformation. What, for example, is the use Dickens makes of sound in *A Christmas Carol*? Such discussions can be particularly rich if group members have transformed the same text into a variety of different media.

DIGESTED READS

Agree in advance on a range of texts that will be covered. These may be primary texts or secondary texts. Each member of the group then takes responsibility for producing a digest of the text they have read on one side of A4. These digests are then circulated to the rest of the group as a useful way in to these texts. The purpose of these digested reads is not to replace the need for reading the original text, but to provide a useful set of key points for consideration, questions, reflections, maybe even suggested activities. These can provide very useful aids to independent study.

As a variant, why not try several people producing digested reads for the same text and comparing the issues they raise – what do they highlight, what do they marginalise, what do they omit altogether?

CAST MEETING

This is another drama-based activity. It is particularly useful for studying drama texts, but would also work well with prose fiction and some poetry. Each member of the group takes on the role of one character from the play/novel/story/poem. They are responsible for explaining in detail how they would seek to portray their character and why. This is then used as a basis for discussion. On a practical note, it is worth electing a director, who will act as chair in the discussion.

A variant of this is to take a particular scene or episode from a text and to discuss this episode in detail, group members focusing on the scene from the perspective of their particular character.

This kind of activity could also work across texts. For example, take an issue which is relevant across an author's work, or across the work of a range of authors. Then select characters from a range of works and have them discuss this issue from their own perspective. This can open up fascinating comparisons and contrasts between texts and can really help you develop the kinds of broad comparative understanding that English Literature degrees demand.

Appendix 2   Recommended reading

It is very hard to make generic recommendations for reading, as English Literature courses at university vary so widely. The English department you are going to attend should supply you with a specific reading list for your first year in advance. It is essential that you use the summer vacation before you begin your course wisely and get ahead with reading, as recommended and outlined in more detail in Chapter 6. It is important, however, as also emphasised in that chapter, that you do not limit your reading exclusively to what you are required to read. Developing your knowledge of English Literature on a wide front will be of inestimable value to you as you progress with your degree and will empower you in many ways, as well as preparing you well for later life.

A useful place to start thinking about developing your wider reading is to return to the Action Plan you drew up in your audit of subject knowledge in Chapter 1. There follows a list of some significant works by each of the named authors to help you make a start. The list also includes the titles of some good introductions to areas such as Literary Theory and the history of English Literature, as well as some general anthologies and course books you may find useful.

LITERARY THEORY AND LITERARY CRITICISM

Barry, P. *Beginning Theory* (2nd ed.).
Bennet, A. and Royle, N. *An Introduction to Literature, Criticism and Theory.*

Brooker, P. and Widdowson, P. *A Practical Reader in Contemporary Literary Theory.*
Culler, J. *Literary Theory: A Very Short Introduction.*
Eaglestone, R. *Doing English* (3rd ed.).
Eagleton, T. *Literary Theory* (2nd ed.).
Eliot, T. S. *Selected Essays.*
Green, K. and LeBihan, J. *Critical Theory and Practice: A Course Book.*
Hawthorn, J. *A Concise Glossary of Contemporary Literary Theory.*
Hopkins, C. *Thinking About Texts.*
Pope, R. *The English Studies Book* (2nd ed.).
Porter Abbot, H. *The Cambridge Introduction to Narrative.*
Rivkin, J. and Ryan, M. (eds) *Literary Theory: An Anthology* (2nd ed.).
Tyson, L. *Critical Theory Today: A User Friendly Guide.*

GENERAL ANTHOLOGIES

The Norton Anthology of English Literature (8th ed.).

GENERAL

Abrams, M. H. *A Glossary of Literary Terms* (6th ed.).
Alexander, M. *A History of English Literature.*
Goring, P., Hawthorn, J. and Mitchell, D. *Studying Literature.*
Sanders, A. *The Short Oxford History of English Literature.*
The Concise Oxford Dictionary.
The Concise Oxford Thesaurus.

CREATIVE WRITING

Bell, J. and Magrs, P. *The Creative Writing Coursebook.*
Earnshaw, S. *The Handbook of Creative Writing.*
Graham, R. et al. (eds) *The Road to Somewhere.*
Lodge, D. *The Art of Fiction.*
May, S. *Doing Creative Writing.*
Mills, P. *The Routledge Creative Writing Coursebook.*
Singleton, J. *The Creative Writing Workbook.*

ENGLISH LANGUAGE

Bailey, R. W. *Images of English.*
Baugh, A. C. and Cable, T. *A History of the English Language.*
Blake, N. F. *A History of the English Language.*
Bragg, M. *The Adventure of English.*
Burchfield, R. *The English Language.*
Bryson, B. *Mother Tongue.*
Carter, R. and Stockwell, P. *The Language and Literature Reader.*
Crystal, D. *The English Language.*
Crystal, D. *The Stories of English.*
Freeborn, D. *From Old English to Standard English.*
McCrum, R. et al. *The Story of English.*
Pennycook, A. *The Cultural Politics of English as an International Language.*
Ricks, C. and Michaels, L. *The State of the Language, 1990s Edition.*
Watts, R. and Trudgill, P. *Alternative Histories of English.*

OLD AND MIDDLE ENGLISH

Burrow, J. A. and Turville-Petre, T. *A Book of Middle English* (6th ed.).

POETRY

Fry, S. *The Ode Less Travelled.*
Hyland, P. *Getting into Poetry.*
Lennard, J. *The Poetry Handbook: A Guide to Reading Poetry for Pleasure and Practical Criticism.*
Matterson, S. and Jones, D. *Studying Poetry.*
Wu, D. (ed.) *Romanticism: A Critical Reader.*

THE NOVEL

Hawthorn, J. *Studying the Novel: An Introduction* (3rd ed.).
Johnson, R. *Studying Fiction: A Guide and Study Programme.*

SHAKESPEARE

Barber, C. L. *Shakespeare's Festive Comedy.*
Bradley, A. C. *Shakespearean Tragedy* (3rd ed.).
Greenblatt, S. *The Norton Shakespeare.*
Kermode, F. *Shakespeare's Language.*
McEvoy, S. *The Basics.*
Palfrey, S. *Doing Shakespeare.*
Ryan, K. *Shakespeare* (3rd ed.).
Tillyard, E. M. W. *Shakespeare's History Plays.*
Wilson Knight, G. *The Wheel of Fire: Interpretations of Shakespearean Tragedy.*
The Riverside Shakespeare.

MAJOR POETS PRE-1914

Matthew Arnold – 'Dover Beach', *Culture and Anarchy, Tristram and Iseult.*
William Blake – *Songs of Innocence and of Experience, Milton, The Marriage of Heaven and Hell.*
Emily Brontë – Collected Poems.
Elizabeth Barrett Browning – *Sonnets from the Portuguese, Aurora Leigh.*
Robert Browning – 'Pippa Passes', 'Porphyria's Lover', 'My Last Duchess', 'Childe Rowland to the Dark Tower Came'.
Robert Burns – *Poems Chiefly in the Scottish Dialect, Tam O'Shanter.*
Lord Byron – *Childe Harold's Pilgrimage, Don Juan, The Corsair.*
Chaucer – *The Canterbury Tales, The Book of the Duchess.*
John Clare – *Poems Descriptive of Rural Life, The Shepherd's Calendar.*
Samuel Taylor Coleridge – *The Rime of the Ancient Mariner, Christabel, Kubla Khan.*
John Donne – *Songs and Sonnets, Holy Sonnets.*
John Dryden – *Annus Mirabilis, Marriage à la Mode, All for Love.*
Thomas Gray – 'Elegy Written in a Country Churchyard', 'Ode on the Spring'.
George Herbert – *The Temple, A Priest to the Temple.*
Robert Herrick – *Hesperides.*
Gerard Manley Hopkins – 'The Wreck of the *Deutschland*', 'The Windhover', 'Binsey Poplars', 'Pied Beauty'.
John Keats – 'Ode to a Nightingale', 'Ode upon a Grecian Urn', 'Endymion', 'La Belle Dame Sans Merci'.

Andrew Marvell – 'To His Coy Mistress', 'The Last Instructions to a Painter'.

John Milton – *Paradise Lost, Paradise Regained*, 'L'Allegro', 'Il Penseroso'.

Alexander Pope – *Essay on Criticism, The Rape of the Lock*, 'Windsor Forest'.

Dante Gabriel Rossetti – *The Blessed Damozel, The Early Italian Poets.*

William Shakespeare – Sonnets, *The Phoenix and the Turtle.*

Percy Bysshe Shelley – *Prometheus Unbound, The Cenci.*

Edmund Spenser – *The Faerie Queene*, 'Epithalamion', 'Amoretti'.

Alfred Lord Tennyson – *Idylls for the King, In Memoriam, Maud and Other Poems.*

Henry Vaughan – Poems.

William Wordsworth – *Lyrical Ballads, The Prelude.*

Thomas Wyatt – Poems.

EXAMPLES OF MAJOR PLAYWRIGHTS

William Congreve – *The Way of the World, The Double Dealer, Love for Love.*

Oliver Goldsmith – *She Stoops to Conquer, The Good-Natured Man.*

Christopher Marlowe – *Doctor Faustus, Tamburlaine the Great, The Jew of Malta.*

Sean O'Casey – *Shadow of a Gunman, Juno and the Paycock.*

Harold Pinter – *The Birthday Party, The Caretaker, The Homecoming.*

J. B. Priestley – *An Inspector Calls, I have Been Here Before, Time and the Conways.*

Peter Shaffer – *Equus, Amadeus.*

George Bernard Shaw – *Pygmalion, Heartbreak House, Mrs Warren's Profession.*

Richard Brinsley Sheridan – *The Rivals, The School for Scandal, The Critic.*

Oscar Wilde – *The Importance of Being Earnest, Lady Windermere's Fan, The Picture of Dorian Gray.*

EXAMPLES OF MAJOR POETS AFTER 1914

W. H. Auden – Collected Shorter Poems, Collected Longer Poems.

Gillian Clarke – *Snow on the Mountain, Letter from a Far Country.*

Keith Douglas – Complete Poems.

T. S. Eliot – *Prufrock and Other Observations, The Waste Land, Four Quartets, Selected Essays.*

U. A. Fanthorpe – *Side Effects, Voices Off, Neck Verse.*

Thomas Hardy – Collected Poems.

Seamus Heaney – *Death of a Naturalist, North, The Haw Lantern, District and Circle, Beowulf, Preoccupations.*

Ted Hughes – *The Hawk in the Rain, Crow, Lupercal, Season Songs, Birthday Letters.*

Elizabeth Jennings – *The Mind has Mountains, Growing Points, Moments of Grace.*

Philip Larkin – *The Whitsun Weddings, The North Ship, High Windows, A Girl in Winter.*

Wilfred Owen – The Complete Poems and Fragments.

Sylvia Plath – *The Colossus and Other Poems, Ariel, The Bell Jar, Johnny Panic and the Bible of Dreams.*

Stevie Smith – *Novel on Yellow Paper, A Good Time Was had by All, Not Waving but Drowning.*

Edward Thomas – Collected Poems.

R. S. Thomas – *Song at the Year's Turning, Tares, The Way of It, Between Here and Now.*

W. B. Yeats – *Cathleen Ni Houlihan, The Wanderings of Oisin and Other Poems, The Green Helmet and other Poems, New Poems.*

EXAMPLES OF FICTION BY MAJOR WRITERS AFTER 1914

E. M. Forster – *Where Angels fear to Tread, A Room with a View, A Passage to India.*

William Golding – *The Lord of the Flies, The Inheritors, Pincher Martin, The Spire, Close Quarters.*

Graham Greene – *The Honorary Consul, Brighton Rock, A Gun for Sale, The Heart of the Matter.*

Aldous Huxley – *Brave New World, Eyeless in Gaza, Ape and Essence.*

James Joyce – *Dubliners, The Portrait of the Artist as a Young Man, Ulysses.*

D. H. Lawrence – *The Rainbow, Women in Love, The Plumed Serpent, Lady Chatterley's Lover.*

Katherine Mansfield – *In a German Pension, Bliss and Other Stories, The Garden Party and Other Stories.*

George Orwell – *Animal Farm, 1984, Down and Out in Paris and London, The Road to Wigan Pier.*

Muriel Spark – *The Comforters, The Ballad of Peckham Rye, The Mandelbaum Gate.*

William Trevor – *The Old Boys, Fools of Fortune, The Children of Dynmouth.*

Evelyn Waugh – *Black Mischief, Scoop, Brideshead Revisited, A Handful of Dust.*

H. G. Wells – *The Island of Dr Moreau, The War of the Worlds, Kipps, Tono-Bungay.*

Virginia Woolf – *The Waves, Mrs Dalloway, To the Lighthouse, Jacob's Room.*

MAJOR FICTION WRITERS PUBLISHED BEFORE 1914

Jane Austen – *Sense and Sensibility, Pride and Prejudice, Persuasion, Emma.*

Charlotte Brontë – *Jane Eyre, Shirley, Villette.*

John Bunyan – *Pilgrim's Progress, Grace Abounding.*

Wilkie Collins – *The Woman in White, The Moonstone, Armadale, No Name.*

Joseph Conrad – *Heart of Darkness, Lord Jim, Victory, Nostromo.*

Daniel Defoe – *Moll Flanders, A Journal of the Plague Year, Robinson Crusoe, Captain Singleton.*

Charles Dickens – *The Pickwick Papers, Nicholas Nickleby, David Copperfield, Hard Times, The Mystery of Edwin Drood.*

Arthur Conan Doyle – *The Hound of the Baskervilles, The Sign of Four, The White Company, Sir Nigel.*

George Eliot – *Silas Marner, The Mill on the Floss, Felix Holt Radical, Middlemarch.*

Henry Fielding – *Joseph Andrews, Jonathan Wild, Tom Jones, Amelia.*

Elizabeth Gaskell – *Cranford, North and South, Mary Barton.*

Thomas Hardy – *The Mayor of Casterbridge, Far from the Madding Crowd, Tess of the d'Urbervilles, Jude the Obscure.*

Henry James – *The Portrait of a Lady, The Wings of the Dove, The American, The Turn of the Screw.*

Rudyard Kipling – *The Jungle Books, Kim, Plain Tales from the Plain Hills.*

Walter Scott – *Kenilworth, Ivanhoe, Rob Roy.*

Mary Shelley – *Frankenstein, The Last Man, Valperga.*

Robert Louis Stevenson – *Treasure Island, Catriona, Kidnapped, The Strange Case of Dr Jeckyll and Mr Hyde.*

Jonathan Swift – *Gulliver's Travels, A Modest Proposal, Verses on His Own Death.*

William Thackeray – *Vanity Fair, The History of Henry Esmond.*

Anthony Trollope – *The Warden, The Last Chronicle of Barset, Phineas Finn, The Little House at Allington.*

British Literature

Peter Ackroyd – *Hawksmoor, Chatterton, First Light, The House of Dr Dee, Blake, Dickens.*

Kingsley Amis – *That Uncertain Feeling, Russian Hide-and-Seek, The Old Devils.*

Martin Amis – *London Fields, Time's Arrow, Money.*

J. G. Ballard – *Empire of the Sun, Crash, Cocaine Nights.*

John Banville – *Nightspawn, The Book of Evidence, The Sea.*

Pat Barker – *Regeneration, The Eye in the Door, The Ghost Road.*

Julian Barnes – *Flaubert's Parrot, A History of the World in 10½ Chapters.*

Malcom Bradbury – *Stepping Westward, The History Man, Dr Criminale.*

Melvyn Bragg – *Without a City Wall, The Maid of Buttermere, A Time to Dance.*

A. S. Byatt – *Possession, The Babel Tower, The Virgin in the Garden.*

Angela Carter – *Wise Children, The Magic Toyshop, The Bloody Chamber.*

Jonathan Coe – *The Accidental Woman, What a Carve Up!, The Dwarves of Death.*

Margaret Drabble – *A Summer Birdcage, Jerusalem the Golden, The Ice Age.*

Sebastian Faulks – *The Girl at the Lion d'Or, Birdsong, Charlotte Gray.*

Susan Hill – *The Woman in Black, The Mist in the Mirror, Strange Meeting.*

Hanif Kureishi – *The Buddha of Suburbia, The Black Album, Love in a Blue Time.*

David Lodge – *Nice Work, Therapy, Small World.*

Andrew Motion – *Larkin, Keats, The Invention of Dr Cake.*

Zadie Smith – *White Teeth, On Beauty.*

Fay Weldon – *The Life and Loves of a She Devil, Down Among the Women, Darcy's Utopia.*
Jeanette Winterson – *Boating for Beginners, The Passion, Oranges Are Not the Only Fruit.*

American Literature

Paul Auster – *New York Trilogy, In the Country of Last Things.*
Saul Bellow – *Herzog, The Adventures of Augie March, Humboldt's Gift.*
Truman Capote – *In Cold Blood, Breakfast at Tiffany's.*
Willa Cather – *O Pioneers!, My Antonia.*
James Fennimore Cooper – *The Last of the Mohicans, The Pioneers, The Prairie.*
John Dos Passos – *USA, Three Soldiers.*
William Faulkner – *As I Lay Dying, Absalom Absalom, The Sound and the Fury.*
F. Scott Fitzgerald – *The Great Gatsby, The Beautiful and the Damned, The Last Tycoon.*
Allen Ginsberg – *Kaddish and Other Poems, Planet News, Poems All Over the Place: Mostly Seventies.*
Nathaniel Hawthorne – *The Scarlet Letter, The House of Seven Gables.*
Ernest Hemingway – *Fiesta, A Movable Feast, A Farewell to Arms, For Whom the Bell Tolls.*
Jack Kerouac – *On the Road, The Subterraneans, Desolation Angels.*
Herman Melville – *Typee, Moby Dick, Billy Budd.*
Arthur Miller – *Death of a Salesman, The Crucible, All My Sons.*
Edgar Allan Poe – *The Murders in the Rue Morgue, The Fall of the House of Usher.*
Ezra Pound – *Lustra, The Cantos, Hugh Selwyn Mauberly.*
Henry Thoreau – *A Week on the Concord and Merrimack Rivers, Walden.*
Walt Whitman – *Memoranda During the War, Leaves of Grass.*
Tennessee Williams – *Cat on a Hot Tin Roof, The Glass Menagerie, A Streetcar Named Desire.*

International Literature

Italo Calvino – *The Cloven Viscount, Building Speculation, Invisible Cities.*
Peter Carey – *Illywhacker, Oscar and Lucinda, Jack Maggs.*
Miguel Cervantes – *Don Quixote, La Galatea.*

J. M. Coetzee – *In the Heart of the Country, Waiting for the Barbarians, Foe.*

Anita Desai – *Fire on the Mountain, In Custody, Journey to Ithaca.*

Fyodor Dostoevsky – *Crime and Punishment, The Brothers Karamazov.*

Alexandre Dumas – *The Three Musketeers, The Count of Monte Cristo, The Man in the Iron Mask.*

Umberto Eco – *The Name of the Rose, The Island of the Day Before, The Mysterious Flame of Queen Loana.*

Gustave Flaubert – *A Sentimental Education, Madame Bovary.*

Nicolai Gogol – *The Government Inspector,* 'Nevsky Prospekt', 'The Nose'.

Franz Kafka – *Metamorphosis, The Castle, The Trial.*

Thomas Keneally – *Three Cheers for the Paraclete, Schindler's Ark, Jacko the Great Intruder.*

Milan Kundera – *The Unbearable Lightness of Being, Life is Elsewhere, Immortality.*

Thomas Mann – *Death in Venice, Tonio Kröger, The Magic Mountain.*

Salman Rushdie – *Midnight's Children, The Moor's Last Sight, Shalimar the Clown.*

Vikram Seth – *A Suitable Boy, Equal Music.*

Stendhal – *The Scarlet and the Black, The Charterhouse of Parma.*

Leo Tolstoy – *War and Peace, Anna Karenina, The Kreutzer Sonata.*

Emil Zola – *Thérèse Raquin, L'Assommoir, Germinal.*

Appendix 3 Literary terms

The following is a list of key literary terms and their definitions. It is important that you are confident, accurate and fluent in your use of technical terminology now that you are operating at degree level. However, it is never sufficient thoughtlessly to drop technical terms into a response to any text; a careful and developed explanation of the impact the effects the author achieves by using the identified technique is essential.

allegory – extended metaphor conveying moral meaning.

alliteration – the use of repeated consonant letter sounds for effect.

allusion – reference, either direct or indirect, to other texts.

anapaest – a metrical foot of three syllables arranged o o ●.

anthropomorphism – literary presentation of the animal world as human.

antithesis – contrast of ideas expressed by parallelism.

apocalypse – the end of the world.

assonance – an imperfect form of rhyme using the same repeated vowel sound but different consonants (e.g. 'man' and 'hat').

bathos – a descent from the elevated to the commonplace.

black humour – humour that makes fun of something serious.

caesura – a natural break falling within the rhythmic line.

caricature – grotesque exaggeration in portrayal of character.

characterisation – the ways in which an author creates and develops a character.

cliché – a worn and over-used expression which has lost its vitality and, to some extent, its original meaning (e.g. 'Oh, play that thing!').

colloquial – the language of common and familiar communication.

connotation – implications that words and phrases carry with them over and above their denotative meaning.

contextuality – historical/cultural/social/economic/political background of a text.

couplet – a pair of consecutive rhyming lines.

dactyl – a metrical foot of three syllables arranged ● ○ ○.

didactic – adjective applied to a work of literature setting out to promote or teach a particular religious, political or philosophical point of view.

dimeter – a line composed of two metrical units or feet.

enjambment – a line of verse or a stanza that runs into the next line or stanza without a break.

end-stopped line – a line 'stopped' at the end by a mark of punctuation.

epigraph – inscription at head of chapter or book.

episodic – when a narrative is divided into individual episodes.

epistolary – taking the form of letters.

feminine rhyme – a rhyme extending over two or more syllables, usually a stressed syllable followed by one or more unstressed syllables.

first person narrative – when a story is told from the 'I' point of view.

genre – type or form of writing.

hexameter – a line composed of six metrical units or feet.

hyperbole – deliberate exaggeration for literary effect.

iamb – a metrical foot of two syllables arranged ○●.

imagery – the use of words to create pictorial images; often appeals to a variety of senses – touch, taste, smell, sight, sound.

internal rhyme – rhyme occurring within a verse or line.

irony – language intended to mean the opposite of the words actually employed; an amusing or cruel reversal of a situation.

juxtaposition – placing ideas/characters/events side by side for contrast (often ironic) or to create other types of literary connection.

litotes – an ironical understatement.

lyric poetry – originally Greek verses sung to the music of the lyre (from the adjective λυρικός).

metaphor – a figure of speech in which a term or phrase is applied to something to which it is not literally applicable.

metre – the more or less regular pattern formed by sequences of syllables.

metrical foot – the way in which units of stressed and unstressed syllables are arranged.

myth – fiction about supernatural beings.

narrative point of view – the point of view expressed by the narrator.

narrative structure – the way in which a story is structured; may be chronological, reverse chronological, episodic, flashbacks and so on.

omniscient narrator – a narrator who has God-like powers to see all events, actions, motivations and thoughts.

oxymoron – an apparently self-contradictory expression used to make a specific point.

parable – a story used to illuminate a moral lesson.

paradox – a seemingly absurd or self-contradictory statement.

pathetic fallacy – use of the weather or the landscape to reflect events/moods/etc.

pathos – sad situation, evoking pity in the reader.

pentameter – a line composed of five metrical units or feet.

persona – a character adopted by an author.

personification – attribution of human qualities to objects, ideas and so on.

plurality – possibility of multiple meanings of text.

prosody – the theory of metre.

pyrrhic – a metrical foot of two syllables arranged oo.

pun – a play on words employing exact aural similarity or likeness.

quatrain – a set of four lines of verse.

register – level of formality in expression.

rhyme – the repetition of same or similar sounds, whether vowels or consonants or a combination in one or more syllables.

rhythm – the movement of language attributable to the pattern of stressed and unstressed syllables.

sestet – a set of six lines of verse.

simile – a comparison of two things having significant resemblance(s) using 'like' or 'as'.

spondee – a metrical foot of two syllables arranged ••.

stereotype – a fixed type of character.

symbolism – use of characters, actions, objects to represent higher, more abstract concepts.

synecdoche – a form of metaphor in which a part (often a body part) is used to represent the whole.

synopsis – summary of plot.

tetrameter – a line composed of four metrical units or feet.

theme – a central or dominating idea of a literary work.

third person narrative – when a story is told from the 'he/she/it' point of view.

tone – the attitude and mood of a literary work and its language.

tragedy – a work of fiction that traces the downfall of a protagonist – often this character is initially seen as 'better' than the rest of us.

trimeter – a line composed of three metrical units or feet.

trochee – a metrical foot of two syllables arranged — ‿.

unreliable narrator – a narrator the reader does not entirely feel able to trust (because of age, naivety, self-delusion, tendency to lie, political reasons, etc.) – this may cover a huge range of reliability.

In the definitions for metrical feet — denotes a stressed syllable and ‿ denotes an unstressed syllable.

Appendix 4 Timeline

Date	Literary period	England	America	Other
800–400 BC	This period was dominated by Greek poets and dramatists.			Homer, Sophocles, and Euripedes.
250 BC–AD 150	Writers of the Roman Empire are most noted in this time period.			Virgil, Horace, and Ovid.
450–1066	Old English (Anglo-Saxon) Period.	*Beowulf* poet; early Bible translations; Bede (c.672–735).		Rise of haiku poetry in Japan.
1066–1500	Middle English Period.	John Gower (c.1330–1408); William Langland (c.1332–1386); Geoffrey Chaucer (1343–1400); The 'Pearl' Poet.		Petrarch (1304–1374); Dante (1307–1321); Boccacio (1313–1375).
1500–1660	The Renaissance Elizabethan (1558–1603) Jacobean (1603–1625) Caroline (1625–1649)	Edmund Spenser (c.1552–1599); Philip Sydney (1554–1586); Christopher Marlowe (1564–1593);	Thomas Morton (c.1576–1647); Anne Bradstreet (c.1612–1672).	Francois Rabelais (1490–1553); Miguel de Cervantes (1547–1616); Moliere (1622–1673);

Date	Literary period	England	America	Other
	Commonwealth (1649–1669)	William Shakespeare (1564–1616); John Donne (1572–1631); Ben Johnson (1572–1637); John Milton (1608–1674); Andrew Marvell (1621–1678); Henry Vaughan (1621–1695).		Madame de Lafayette (1634–1693).
1660–1785	The Neoclassical Period The Restoration (1660–1700) The Augustan Age (1700–1745).	Daniel Defoe (1660–1731); Jonathan Swift (1667–1745); Alexander Pope (1688–1744); Samuel Johnson (1709–1784); Horace Walpole (1717–1797).	Cotton Mather (1663–1728); Jonathan Edwards (1703–1758); Benjamin Franklin (1706–1790); Phillis Wheatley (1753–1784).	Voltaire (1694–1778); Jean-Jacques Rousseau (1712–1778); Denis Diderot (1713–1784).
1785–1830	The Romantic Period The Gothic Period (c.1785–1820, though it lasted longer in America).	William Blake (1757–1827); William Wordsworth (1770–1850); Samuel Taylor Coleridge (1772–1834); Jane Austen (1775–1817); Thomas de Quincey (1785–1859); Lord Byron (1788–1824); Percy Bysshe Shelley (1792–1822);	James Fenimore Cooper (1789–1851); Olaudah Equiano (c.1745–1797); Charles Brockden Brown (1771–1810); Washington Irving (1783–1859); Philip Freneau (1752–1832).	Choderlos de Laclos (1741–1803); Johann Wolfgang von Goethe (1749–1832); Friedrich Johann von Schiller (1759–1805); Stendhal (1783–1842); Heinrich Heine (1797–1856);

Date	Literary period	England	America	Other
		John Keats (1795–1821); Mary Shelley (1797–1851).		Alexander Pushkin (1799–1837); Honore de Balzac (1799–1850).
1830–1901	The Victorian Period 1848–1860 The Pre-Raphaelites 1840–1860 Transcendentalism (America) 1865–1900 Age of Realism (America)	Elizabeth Barrett Browning (1806–1861); Alfred, Lord Tennyson (1809–1892); William Makepeace Thackeray (1811–1863); Charles Dickens (1812–1870); Robert Browning (1812–1889); Anthony Trollope (1815–1882); Charlotte Bronte (1816–1855); Emily Bronte (1818–1848); George Eliot (a.k.a. Marian Evans) (1819–1880); Matthew Arnold (1822–1888); Wilkie Collins (1824–1889);	Ralph Waldo Emerson (1803–1882); Nathaniel Hawthorne (1804–1864); Edgar Allan Poe (1809–1849); Harriet Jacobs (1813–1897); Henry David Thoreau (1817–1862); Frederick Douglass (1818–1895); Herman Melville (1819–1891); Walt Whitman (1819–1892); Emily Dickinson (1830–1886); Mark Twain (a.k.a. Samuel Clemens) (1835–1910); Henry James (1843–1916); Kate Chopin (1850–1904); Stephen Crane (1871–1900).	Alexandre Dumas (1802–1870); Victor Hugo (1802–1885); Nikolai Gogol (1809–1852); Charles Baudelaire (1821–1867); Fyodor Dostoevsky (1821–1881); Gustave Flaubert (1821–1880); Edmond de Goncourt (1822–1896); Jules de Goncourt (1830–1870) Jules Verne (1828–1905); Henrik Ibsen (1828–1906); Leo Tolstoy (1828–1910); Emil Zola (1840–1902); Stephane Mallarme (1842–1898); Benito Perez Galdos (1843–1920);

Date	Literary period	England	America	Other
		Gerard Manley Hopkins (1844–1889); George Gissing (1857–1903).		August Strindberg (1849–1912); Guy de Maupassant (1850–1893).
1901–1945	The Modern Period	Joseph Conrad (1857–1924); W.B. Yeats (1865–1939); Ford Madox Ford (1873–1939); E.M. Forster (1879–1970); James Joyce (1882–1941); Virginia Woolf (1882–1941); D.H. Lawrence (1885–1930); Siegfried Sassoon (1886–1967); Wilfred Owen (1893–1918); George Orwell (1903–1950); W.H. Auden (1907–1973); Malcolm Lowry (1909–1957).	Edith Wharton (1862–1937); Willa Cather (1873–1947); Robert Frost (1874–1963); Jack London (1876–1916); Ezra Pound (1885–1972); T.S. Eliot (1888–1965); Zora Neale Hurston (1891–1960); Edna St. Vincent Millay (1892–1950); F. Scott Fitzgerald (1896–1940); William Faulkner (1897–1962); Ernest Hemingway (1899–1961); John Steinbeck (1902–1968); Tennessee Williams (1911–1983).	Luigi Pirandello (1867–1936); Andre Gide (1869–1951); Marcel Proust (1871–1922); Rainer Maria Rilke (1875–1926); Thomas Mann (1875–1955); Fillippo Marinetti (1876–1944); Herman Hesse (1877–1962); Alexander Blok (1880–1921); Franz Kafka (1883–1924); Katharine Mansfield (1888–1923); Boris Pasternak (1890–1960); Mikhail Bulgakov (1891–1940); Jean-Paul Sartre (1905–1980);

Date	Literary period	England	America	Other
				Simone de Beauvoir (1908–1986); Albert Camus (1913–1960).
1950–	Postmodernism	William Golding (1911–1993); Lawrence Durrell (1912–1990); Philip Larkin (1922–1985); Kingsley Amis (1922–1995); John Fowles (1926–2005); Ted Hughes (1930–1998); Harold Pinter (1930–2008); Fay Weldon (1931–); A.S. Byatt (1936–); Samuel Beckett (1906–1989); Seamus Heaney (1939–); Angela Carter (1940–1992); Susan Hill (1942–); John Banville (1945–); Julian Barnes (1946–); Salman Rushdie (1947–); Peter Ackroyd (1949–);	Eugene O'Neill (1888–1953); Ralph Ellison (1914–1994); Arthur Miller (1915–2005); J.D. Salinger (1919–); Ray Bradbury (1920–); Jack Kerouac (1922–1969); Joseph Heller (1923–1999); Maya Angelou (1928–); Toni Morrison (1931–); Sylvia Plath (1932–1963); Philip Roth (1933–); Maxine Hong Kingston (1940–); Alice Walker (1944–); Charles Palliser (1947–); Amy Tan (1952–); Sandra Cisneros (1954–).	Eugene Ionesco (1909–1994); Jean Genet (1910–1986); Patrick White (1912–1990); Heinrich Boll (1917–1985); Italo Calvino (1923–1985); Gunther Grass (1927–); Elie Wiesel (1928–); Milan Kundera (1929–); Chinua Achebe (1930–); Umberto Eco (1932–); Athol Fugard (1932–); Akinwande Soyinka (1934–); Thomas Keneally (1935–); J.M. Coetzee (1940–); Peter Carey (1943–).

Date	Literary period	England	America	Other
		Martin Amis (1949–); Andrew Motion (1952–); Jeanette Winterson (1959–); Jonathan Coe (1961–); Zadie Smith (1975–).		

Bibliography

Ackroyd, P. *Blake*. London: Sinclair-Stevenson, 1995.

Ackroyd, P. *Hawksmoor*. London: Hamish Hamilton, 1985.

Ackroyd, P. *The House of Dr Dee*. London: Hamish Hamilton, 1993.

Ania, L. *Colonialism/Postcolonialism*. London: Routledge, 1998.

Anonymous. *Beowulf*. Seamus Heaney (trans.). London: Faber & Faber, 1999.

Anonymous. *Pearl*. E.V. Gordon (ed.). Oxford: Clarendon Press, 1953.

Anonymous. *Sir Gawain and the Green Knight*. Simon Armitage (trans.). London: Faber & Faber, 2006.

Ashcroft, B. et al. *Key Concepts in Post-Colonial Studies*. London: Routledge, 1998.

Ashcroft, B. et al. *The Post-Colonial Studies Reader*. London: Routledge, 1995.

Austen, J. *Pride and Prejudice*. London: Penguin, 2003.

Auerbach, E. *Mimesis: The Representation of Reality in Western Literature*. Willard Trask (trans.). Princeton: Princeton University Press, 1953.

Bailey, R.W. *Images of English*. Cambridge: Cambridge University Press, 1992.

Bakhtin, M. *The Dialogic Imagination: Four Essays*. M. Holquist (ed.). C. Emerson and M. Holquist (trans.). Austin: Texas University Press, 1981.

Baldick, C. *The Concise Oxford Dictionary of Literary Terms*. Oxford: Oxford University Press, 2001.

Barber, C.L. *Shakespeare's Festive Comedy*. New Jersey: Princeton University Press, 1959.

Barker, P. *Regeneration*. London: Penguin, 1990.

Barry, P. *Beginning Theory*, 2nd edition. Manchester: Manchester University Press, 2002.

Baugh, A.C. and Cable, T. *A History of the English Language*. London: Routledge, 2002.

Beckett, S. *The Collected Works of Samuel Beckett: Waiting for Godot*, 3rd edition. New York: Grove Press, 1978.

Belsey, C. and Moore, J. (eds). *The Feminist Reader: Essays in Gender and the Politics of Literary Criticism*. London: Macmillan, 1989.

Bennet, A. and Royle, N. *An Introduction to Literature, Criticism and Theory*. Hemel Hempstead: Prentice Hall/Harvester Wheatshaft, 2004.

Blake, N.F. *A History of the English Language*. London: Palgrave, 1996.

Blake, W. *Complete Writings*. Geoffrey Keynes (ed.). Oxford: Oxford University Press, 1972.

Blessington, F. *Paradise Lost and the Classical Epic*. London: Routledge, 1979.

Bliss, A. *Morning Heroes*. London: EMI Classics, 2007.

Bolgan, A. *What the Thunder Really Said*. Montreal: McGill-Queen's University Press, 1973.

Botting, F. *Gothic: The New Critical Idiom*. London: Routledge, 1996.

Brecht, B. *Mother Courage and Her Children*. London: Methuen, 1983.

Brittain, V. *Testament of Youth*. London: Penguin, 1994.

Britten, B. *War Requiem*. London: Decca, 2006.

Bronte, E. *Wuthering Heights*. London: Penguin, 2003.

Brown, D. *Angels and Demons*. London: Corgi, 2001.

Burchfield, R. *The English Language*. Oxford: Oxford University Press, 2002.

Burke, E. *A Philosophical Enquiry into the Origin of Our Ideas of the Sublime and Beautiful*. Oxford: Oxford University Press, 2008.

Burrow, C. *Epic Romance: Homer to Milton*. Oxford: Clarendon Press, 1993.

Byatt, A.S. *Possession*. London: Chatto & Windus, 1990.

Byron, Lord. *The Major Works*. Oxford: Oxford University Press, 2000.

Carter, R. and Stockwell, P. *The Language and Literature Reader*. London: Routledge, 2008.

Chaucer, G. *The Riverside Chaucer*, 3rd edition. Oxford: Oxford University Press, 1988.

Childs, P. and Fowler, R. (eds). *The Routledge Dictionary of Literary Terms*. New York: Routledge, 2005.

Chrisman, L. and Williams, P. *Colonial Discourse and Post-Colonial Theory: A Reader*. Hemel Hempstead: Harvester, 1993.

Coetzee, J.M. *Foe*. London: Penguin, 1987.

Cohen, W. 'The Merchant of Venice and the possibilities of historical criticism', in Ivo Kamps (ed.) *Materialist Shakespeare: A History*. London: Verso, 1995.

Collins, W. *Armadale*. Oxford: Oxford University Press, 1989.

Collins, W. *The Moonstone*. Oxford: Oxford University Press, 2008.

Collins, W. *The Woman in White*. London: Penguin, 1987.

Conrad, J. *Heart of Darkness*. London: Penguin, 2000.

Crystal, D. *The English Language*. London: Penguin, 2002.

Cuddon, J.A. *The Penguin Dictionary of Literary Terms and Literary Theory*. London: Penguin Books, 1991.

Culler, J. *On Deconstruction: Theory and Criticism After Structuralism*. London: Routledge, 1983.

Culler, J. *Saussure*. London: Fontana, 1990.

Culler, J. *The Pursuit of Signs: Semiotics, Literature, Deconstruction*. London: Routledge, 1993.

Davies, T. and Wood, N. (eds). *The Waste Land*. Buckingham: Open University Press, 1994.

Defoe, D. *Robinson Crusoe*. London: Penguin, 2004.

Dickens, C. *A Tale of Two Cities*. London: Penguin, 2003.

Dickens, C. *David Copperfield*. London: Penguin, 2004.

Dickens, C. *Great Expectations*. London: Penguin, 2004.

Dickens, C. *Hard Times*. London: Penguin, 2007.

Dickens, C. *Nicholas Nickelby*. London: Penguin, 2003.

Dickens, C. *The Mystery of Edwin Drood*. London: Penguin, 2003.

Docherty, T. *Postmodernism: A Reader*. London: Harvester Wheatsheaf, 1993.

Dollimore, J. and Sinfield, A. 'History and ideology: Henry V', in Graham Holderness (ed.) *Shakespeare's History Plays*. London: Macmillan, 1992.

Dos Passos, J. *Three Soldiers*. London: Penguin, 1999.

Eagleton, M. (ed.). *Feminist Literary Theory: A Reader*. Oxford: Blackwell, 1986.

Eagleton, T. *Marxism and Literary Criticism*. London: Routledge, 1989.

Eliot, G. *Middlemarch*. London: Penguin, 2003.

Eliot, T.S. *The Waste Land*. London: Faber & Faber, 2002.

Empson, W. *Milton's God*. Cambridge: Cambridge University Press, 1965.

Faulks, S. *Birdsong*. London: Vintage, 1994.

Fernie, E. *Shame in Shakespeare*. London: Routledge, 2002.

Fitzgerald, F.S. *The Great Gatsby*. London: Penguin, 2000.

Ford, F.M. *The Good Soldier: A Tale of Passion*. London: Penguin, 2007.

Freeborn, D. *From Old English to Standard English*. London: Macmillan, 2002.

Freud, S. *The Interpretation of Dreams*. Oxford: Oxford University Press, 2008.

Gardner, H. *Frames of Mind: The Theory of Multiple Intelligences*. New York: Basic, 1983.

Gibson, A. 'Badiou and Beckett', in Richard Lane (ed.) *Beckett and Philosophy*. London: Macmillan, 2002.

Gower, J. *Confessio Amantis*. London: Penguin, 1963.

Green, A. 'A desk and a pile of books: Considering independent study'. *Pedagogy*. Volume 7 (3): 427–452, 2007.

Green, A. *Four Perspectives on Transition: English Literature from Sixth Form to University*. Higher Education Academy English Subject Centre: Royal Holloway, University of London, 2005.

Green, M. and Kingsbury, I. *How to Write a Successful University Personal Statement Application*. Nottingham: Apply2 Limited, 2007.

Hall, S. (ed.). *The Empire Strikes Back: Race and Racism in 70s Britain*. London: Hutchinson, 1982.

Hamilton, P. *Historicism*. London: Routledge, 1996.

Hasek, J. *The Good Soldier Svejk*. London: Penguin, 2005.

Hawkes, T. *Structuralism and Semiotics*. London: Methuen, 1977.

Heaney, S. *North*. London: Faber & Faber, 2001.

Hemingway, E. *A Farewell to Arms*. London: Vintage, 2005.

Hill, S. *The Mist in the Mirror*. London: Longman, 1995.

Hill, S. *The Woman in Black*. London: Vintage, 2007.

Hill, S. *Strange Meeting*. London: Penguin, 1982.

Holderness, G. (ed.). *Shakespeare's History Plays*. London: Macmillan, 1992.

Homer. *Iliad*. London: Penguin, 2003.

Hutcheon, L. *The Politics of Postmodernism*. London: Routledge, 2002.

James, H. *The Turn of the Screw and Other Stories*. Oxford: Oxford University Press, 2008.

James, M.R. *Count Magnus and Other Ghost Stories*. London: Penguin, 2006.

Jameson, F. *The Prison House of Language: A Critical Account of Structuralism and Russian Formalism*. Princeton: Princeton University Press, 1973.

Joyce, J. *Ulysses*. London: Penguin, 2000.

Keats, J. *Major Works*. Oxford: Oxford University Press, 2001.

Kennedy, X.J., Dana G. and Bauerlein, M. *The Longman Dictionary of Literary Terms: Vocabulary for the Informed Reader*. New York: Pearson/Longman, 2006.

Kolb, D. *Experiential Learning*. Englewood Cliffs, NJ: Prentice Hall, 1984.

Kress, G. 'Interrelations of reading and writing', in A. Wilkinson (ed.). *The Writing of Writing*. Milton Keynes: Open University Press. pp. 198–214, 1986.

Langland, W. *Piers Plowman*. Oxford: Oxford University Press, 2000.

Larkin, P. *High Windows*. London: Faber & Faber, 1979.

Larkin, P. *The Whitsun Weddings*. London: Faber & Faber, 2001.

Lawrence, D.H. *The Rainbow*. London: Penguin, 2007.

Lewis, M. *The Monk*. Oxford: Oxford University Press, 2008.

Lewis, W. *Tarr*. London: Penguin, 1989.

Marx, K. *Das Kapital*. London: Penguin, 2004.

McCrum, R. et al. *The Story of English*. London: Faber, 1992.

Milton, J. *Paradise Lost*. London: Penguin, 2003.

Moi, T. *Sexual/Textual Politics*. London: Routledge, 2002.

Norris, C. *Deconstruction: Theory and Practice*. London: Routledge, 2002.

Patterson, A. *Shakespeare and the Popular Voice*. Oxford: Blackwell, 1989.

Peake, M. *Gormenghast*. London: Vintage, 2007.

Pennycook, A. *The Cultural Politics of English as an International Language*. London: Longman, 1994.

Pope, A. *Rape of the Lock*. London: Vintage, 2007.

Potter, D. *The Singing Detective*. London: Faber & Faber, 2003.

Punter, D. *The Literature of Terror*, 2nd edition. Harlow: Longman, 1996.

Rackin, P. *Stages of History: Shakespeare's English Chronicles*. Ithaca: Cornell University Press, 1990.

Radcliffe, A. 'On the supernatural in poetry'. *New Monthly Magazine*. Volume 16(1): 145–152, 1826.

Radcliffe, A. *The Italian*. London: Penguin, 2005.

Radcliffe, A. *The Mysteries of Udolpho*. London: Penguin, 2006.

Remarque, E.M. *All Quiet on the Western Front*. London: Vintage, 1996.

Ricks, C. and Michaels, L. *The State of the Language, 1990s Edition*. London: Faber, 1990.

Rivkin, J. and Ryan, M. (eds). *Literary Theory: An Anthology*, 2nd edition. Oxford: Blackwell, 2004.

Robey, D. (ed.). *Structuralism: An Introduction*. Oxford: Clarendon Press, 1979.

Rootham, C. *For the Fallen*. London: EMI Classics, 2007.

Ryan, K. *Shakespeare*. Hemel Hempstead: Prentice Hall, 1991.

Said, E. *Culture and Imperialism*. London: Chatto & Windus, 1996.

Said, E. *Orientalism*, 2nd edition. London: Penguin, 1995.

Sassoon, S. *Memoirs of an Infantry Officer*. London: Faber & Faber, 1974.

Shakespeare, W. *As You Like It*. London: Arden, 2004.

Shakespeare, W. *Coriolanus*. London: Arden, 1976.

Shakespeare, W. *Hamlet*. London: Arden, 2005.

Shakespeare, W. *Henry IV Part 1*. London: Arden, 1996.

Shakespeare, W. *Henry V*. London: Arden, 1997.

Shakespeare, W. *King Lear*. London: Arden, 1997.

Shakespeare, W. *Macbeth*. London: Arden, 2001.

Shakespeare, W. *Othello*. London: Arden, 2001.

Shakespeare, W. *The Merchant of Venice*. Martin Coyle (ed.). London: Macmillan, 1998.

Shakespeare, W. *The Tempest*. London: Arden, 2000.

Shakespeare, W. *Timon of Athens*. London: Arden, 2008.

Shakespeare, W. *Titus Andronicus*. London: Arden, 1995.

Shakespeare, W. *Twelfth Night*. London: Arden, 2008.

Shapiro, J. *Shakespeare and the Jews*. New York: Columbia University Press, 1996.

Shelley, M. *Frankenstein*. London: Penguin, 2004.

Shelley, M. *The Last Man*. Oxford: Oxford University Press, 2008.

Shelley, M. *Valperga*. Oxford: Oxford University Press, 2000.

Shelley, P.B. *The Major Works*. Oxford: Oxford University Press, 2003.

Spenser, E. *Faerie Queene*. London: Penguin, 2007.

Stannard, I. *How to Write a Winning UCAS Personal Statement*. London: The Daily Telegraph, 2008.

Stevenson, D. *1914–1918: The History of the First World War*. London: Penguin Press, 2004.

Telfer, P. *Personal Statements: How to Write a UCAS Personal Statement*. London: Iris Books, 2005.

Tompkins, J.P. (ed.). *Reader-Response Criticism: From Formalism to Post-Structuralism*. Baltimore: Johns Hopkins, 1980.

Trollope, A. *Phineas Finn*. London: Penguin, 2006.

Trollope, A. *The Last Chronicle of Barset*. London: Penguin, 2006.

Trollope, A. *The Warden*. London: Penguin, 2004.

Virgil, *Aeneid*. London: Penguin, 2003.

Walcott, D. *Omeros*. London: Faber & Faber, 2002.

Walpole, H. *The Castle of Otranto*. London: Penguin, 2007.

Watts, R. and Trudgill, P. *Alternative Histories of English*. London: Routledge, 2002.

Williams, R. *Marxism and Literature*. Oxford: OUP, 1983.

Wilson, A. *The Victorians*. London: Hutchinson, 2002.

Wood, N. (ed.). *Theory in Practice: Henry IV*. Buckingham: Open University Press, 1995.

Wright, E. *Psychoanalytic Criticism: Theory in Practice*. London: Methuen, 1984.

Zizek, S. *Looking Awry: An Introduction to Jacques Lacan through Popular Culture*. Cambridge Mass.: MIT Press, 1993.

Index